Aldo Zilli

The Zilli Cookbook

Aldo Zilli

SIMON & SCHUSTER
A VIACOM COMPANY

First published in Great Britain by Simon & Schuster UK Ltd, 2003
A Viacom Company

This edition produced for The Book People Ltd, Hall Wood Avenue, Haydock, St Helens WA11 9UL

Simon & Schuster UK Ltd
Africa House
64–78 Kingsway
London WC2B 6AH

1 3 5 7 9 10 8 6 4 2

Design and typesetting: Fiona Andreanelli
Photography: Steve Baxter
Styling for food photography: Liz Belton
Food stylist: David Morgan

Printed and bound in China

ISBN 0 7432 4009 X

To my mom, Maria, the person who inspired me to cook and work hard in my life and Marisa, my sister-in-law, who picked up all my mother's recipes and cooked them for me, and her husband, Giacomo.

Acknowledgements

My biggest thanks go to my extremely understanding personal assistant, Luisa, who works wonders with my scribbles.

A big thank you to Peter Osbourne for tasting and trying all the recipes.

Special thanks to Avv. Benigno D'Orazio, Presidente Commissione Bilancio for the Abruzzo Region, who organised our trip to the region to take photographs for the book. Also, thanks to Nicola Pellicciotta for all the contacts he provided.

Contents

Introduction

Writing books is a bit like opening a restaurant, except that with books you can sit back when you have finished, while with restaurants (of which I own four) it is a 24-hour job! This is my fourth book and by now I know what English people love about Italian food, so I have tried to keep the recipes simple and creative. I am a lover of good food and wines and this great book has given me the opportunity to share my passion for cooking with you at home.

This book is a bit of a culinary journey, both in and around Italy and the recipes I inherited from my family.

When I was 12 my mom decided that I was going to help her in the kitchen. The poor woman had eight boys and one girl, and I was the youngest. I was rather spoilt, not with wealth, but with the love that she gave me every day of my life, until she left us. My early memories are of her working with dad on the farm, milking the cows at 6 a.m. so we would have fresh milk before going to school. After this, she would go and pick vegetables and kill a chicken for lunch or make an amazing sauce for the pasta, which she also made herself.

She never went food shopping because all the produce was grown at home and she made the best of whatever she had, making cheese from cow's or goat's milk, using olive oil from our olive tree and wine from our vineyard. At Christmas my dad would ask us to help him kill a big pig and I would help my mother make sausages and salami and cure the hams. I'll never forget covering the hams with sea salt and putting them in our loft for 12 months so we would be self-sufficient as far as food was concerned.

It was a huge shock when my dad came home one day and told us we were moving from the farm. He had bought a big house, which was great news, but it wasn't a farm or anything like, but a place by the sea, far from the home-grown produce I was used to. My shock was nothing compared to that of my mother. Imagine: she would no longer have fields full of fruit and vegetables, or cows, and no pig at Christmas. Suddenly life was expensive. To make ends meet the whole family had to find jobs, so at half-term I helped the local fisherman, who paid me with fish at the end of the day. It wasn't very glamorous but it felt good being able to feed the family at the age of 13. By now I was making pasta and fish sauces with mom and on Sundays, instead of going to church (one of my brothers is a priest), I would help in the kitchen making gnocchi and roasting a nice sea bass. Then, my mother and I would go to the evening mass instead.

At the farm we took for granted all the wonderful ingredients we had. Now, suddenly, I was missing all the food my mother cooked, the great meat, rabbit, chicken, and wild boar, although our diet became a lot lighter with lots of fish.

My biggest food culture shock was when I went abroad, first stop Munich, where Italian restaurants were getting away with murder — oily sauces, overcooked pasta and over-done fish! The change was too much for me. I only lasted a year before going home to work in the local hotels. As winter came, the hotels shut down and off I went again. I planned to go to London for a couple of weeks holiday and many years later I am still here.

When I first arrived in London, full of enthusiasm but missing my mom a lot, I had to work to send money home because I didn't want her to struggle anymore. It was difficult, but eventually I found work in an Italian restaurant. The owner was a chef, so the food was okay, but nothing like what I was used to. I remember trying to find some olive oil and the only place I could get it was from a chemist. I longed for the food from my family's farm, but I needed money so I adapted, making prawn cocktails, chicken Kiev, spaghetti Bolognese, oily lasagne and cannelloni. I moved from restaurant to restaurant until one day the owner of one restaurant recognised my talent and said "Aldo, I want to retire. Do you want to franchise my restaurant?" Of course, I jumped at the chance and soon made a great success of it by changing the menu to a lighter Italian style of cooking, with more fish and light sauces for pasta. People in the

media started coming to my restaurant, as well as celebrities. My success spread by word of mouth and soon my restaurant was full. I would go to the fish market every morning, then the vegetable market, and gradually I started importing more and more from Italy.

Before I finish I would like to recommend some places in my beautiful home region of Abruzzo, as it is so easy to get there now with direct flights to Pescara. Starting with restaurants: if you go to a fish restaurant in this region you don't get a menu, so try to avoid the places where you see menus with English translations. Usually, they are right on the beach. The ones further inland are the best for food and value for money. La Regina, which is in the centre of Pescara, averages £20 a head. L'Angolino (tel 0872 61632), currently the best restaurant in Abruzzo for fish, is not cheap but worth every penny and the little drive from Pescara. The address is Maria di San Vito Chietino Via Sangritana and booking is recommended, but remember it is closed on Mondays. Another good fish restaurant is Old Marine, which is 20 minutes from Pescara. I would also recommend La Conchiglia d'Oro in Pineto (tel 0859 492333). The chefs, Di Remignio Claudio and Di Nicola Antonio, do a great job. The Locanda Mantone Taverna 58 is the best restaurant for meat in Pescara. Also in Pescara I visited La Lumaca Restaurant (tel 0854 510880). You must book! It probably has the best cellar in the region with a wine for every course – a fantastic, fun place. Another heavenly place has to be Azienda Agriverde with a few rooms and mamma in the kitchen cooking with the best home-grown, organic ingredients (tel 0859 039054), 45 minutes from Pescara airport.

Less than half an hours drive north of Pescara you get to a village called Giulianova, which is near my village, and there you will find my favourite hotel, the Don Juan. On the same stretch of coastline near the hotel is a fantastic fish restaurant called Osteria Dal Moro (tel 0858 004973), which is closed on Wednesdays. It is all fish and wonderful pasta and is not expensive.

Now let's talk about my village, Alba Adriatica, which has many hotels. I will only recommend a couple: the Hotel Meripol and Hotel Impero. We also have the best organic restaurant in the region, called L'Arca, in the centre of the village. Don't miss the Monday market and the best pizza place called La Fattoria.

Recommended hotels in the region include: Mion Hotel Silve Marina, by the sea (tel 0859 350935); Sporting Hotel Villa Maria, in the hills (tel 0854 511001); Aquario Hotel in Vasto (tel 0873 801986); Hotel Villa Dragonetti L'Aquila (tel 0862 680222); Castello Chiola (a converted castle) in the historical town of Loreto Aprutino (tel 0858 290690); and Montinope Hotel Cooking School, in the Pescara hills (tel 0854 962836).

All that is left is to say thank you for giving me the chance I would never have had in my own country. So, *buon appetite* and god bless your supper.

Antipasti

This course was very popular in the old days in the Italian household; they used to have lots of **antipasti** on the table so when they sat down they didn't have to wait for the food. Then came the pasta, the main course and maybe dessert. Nowadays people eat a lot less, so maybe this course has become the **first course** in place of pasta.

But with this great word you can associate cold meats, roasted vegetables, marinated olives, polenta, wild mushrooms, cheese of any kind – and then there is **antipasti di pesce** which of course means **fish hors d'oeuvres**. This could range from a simple seafood salad to clams in wine and garlic, mussels, oysters, prawns or any kind of shellfish, simply marinated in some olive oil and lemon. In the region of Puglia, people are eating more and more raw fish, and during my last visit to the region I was presented with some scallops and squid in lemon oil, salt and parsley, which was very good. But you must make absolutely sure that your fish is very fresh or the fisherman is **a good mate** before you start dealing in raw fish.

Adriatic Fish Soup
Zuppa di Pesce dell' Adriatico

Serves 4   Preparation time: 30 minutes + 30 minutes soaking
Cooking time: 45 minutes

500 g (1 lb 2 oz) clams or mussels

60 ml (4 tablespoons) olive oil

2 garlic cloves, chopped finely

1 shallot, chopped finely

450 g (1 lb) red mullet or cod fillets

850 ml (1½ pints) fish stock

500 g (1 lb 2 oz) squid, cleaned and cut in rings

150 ml (¼ pint) white wine

400 g can of borlotti beans, drained and rinsed

225 g (8 oz) medium-sized raw prawns, peeled and veins removed

leaves of 1 fresh rosemary sprig, chopped

5 ml (1 teaspoon) chopped fresh coriander

5 ml (1 teaspoon) chopped fresh flat-leaf parsley

15 ml (1 tablespoon) cornflour

30 ml (2 tablespoons) cold water

5 ml (1 teaspoon) salt

5 ml (1 teaspoon) freshly ground black pepper

juice of 1 lime

1. If using clams, soak them in salted water for 30 minutes to remove the grit, then wash in clean water and drain. If using mussels, scrub them clean and remove the beards and barnacles. Discard any open ones.

2. Heat half of the oil in a heavy-based deep pan and sauté the garlic and shallot for 3 minutes until just golden. Add the mullet or cod and cook over a medium heat for 3 minutes, before adding the stock. Simmer for 20 minutes.

3. Meanwhile, put the clams or mussels, squid and wine in another large, heavy-based pan. Cover tightly and cook over a high heat for 3–5 minutes, shaking the pan frequently, until the shells have opened.

4. Strain the pan juices through a fine sieve, then add to the squid. Add the beans to the squid and simmer for 5–8 minutes.

5. Meanwhile, remove the shells from the mussels or clams, discarding any that have remained closed. Stir the mussels or clams, prawns, rosemary, coriander, parsley and the remaining oil into the squid mixture. Simmer for a further 10 minutes.

6. Mix together the cornflour and water to form a paste and add it to the mixture. Stir over a gentle heat for 2 minutes until the soup is just thickened and no longer cloudy. Season to taste with salt and black pepper and lime juice.

7. Ladle the soup into four warmed bowls and serve immediately, with warm ciabatta bread.

Goat's Cheese & Herb Soufflé
Soufflé al Formaggio di Capra

Serves 4   Preparation time: 10 minutes   Cooking time: 30 minutes

A soufflé is everyone's nightmare so, for you at home, I have chosen a really simple one. In this recipe dolcelatte or even Cheddar cheese can be substituted for the goat's cheese. You could also add some spinach, which will give it a lovely colour.

30 g (generous 1 oz) butter, plus extra for greasing

30 g (generous 1 oz) plain flour

300 ml (½ pint) full-cream milk

5 eggs, separated (use only 4 yolks)

200 g (7 oz) goat's cheese, chopped

30 ml (2 tablespoons) chopped fresh mixed herbs, e.g. parsley, basil and thyme

salt and freshly ground black pepper

1. In a saucepan, melt the butter and stir in the flour. Leave to cook for 1 minute. Then slowly add the milk to make a white sauce. Bring to the boil and simmer over a very low heat for 3 minutes, then allow to cool slightly.

2. Stir in four of the egg yolks and the goat's cheese and stir until melted and smooth. Add the herbs and season to taste. You can prepare up to this stage ahead of time. Both the cheese mixture and the egg whites will keep for several hours in the refrigerator so long as they are covered with clingfilm.

3. Preheat the oven to 200°C/fan oven 180°C/Gas Mark 6. Butter a 1.2-litre (2-pint) soufflé dish and tie a piece of buttered greaseproof or parchment paper around the outside, extending at least 5 cm (2 inches) above the rim.

4. In a bowl, whisk the five egg whites until they are stiff. Stir half of the egg whites into the soufflé mixture to loosen it. Then fold in the rest of the egg whites using a metal spoon.

5. Pour the mixture into a soufflé dish. Bake until the soufflé is risen and golden brown – this will take about 25 minutes – and serve immediately.

Roasted Pecorino Cheese with Honey & Italian Sausages
Pecorino Arrostito al Miele e Salsiccia

Serves 4   Preparation time: 10 minutes   Cooking time: 20 minutes

For this recipe you really need to visit an Italian deli, to make sure the sausages and pecorino are of the very best quality. This is a very peasanty sort of recipe that farm workers used to eat for mid morning breakfast. In Italy in those days nobody used to have breakfast as such. You got up, had an espresso and then went to work and if you were nearby at about 9.30 you would go home and mamma would have prepared this wonderful recipe with lots of fresh bread just baked – not bad. Today, this makes a great starter.

60 ml (4 tablespoons) plain flour
250 g (9 oz) hard, fresh pecorino cheese
8 Italian spicy pork sausages
60 ml (4 tablespoons) olive oil
1 fresh red chilli, de-seeded and chopped finely
2 garlic cloves, chopped finely
4 teaspoons of good honey
salt and freshly ground black pepper

1. Sprinkle the flour on to a plate and season it. Cut the pecorino into fish-finger-size pieces and roll in the flour.

2. Pierce the sausages with a fork so when you are cooking them all the excess fat will come out. Place on a baking tray or roasting tin with a tablespoon of the olive oil and roast for 15 minutes. Then cover with foil and cook for a further 5 minutes.

3. Meanwhile, in a non–stick frying pan, cook the cheese in 30 ml (2 tablespoons) of the olive oil for about 2 minutes each side or until it starts to melt. Take out the cheese and place on some kitchen paper to drain.

4. To the same pan, add the remaining olive oil, the chilli, garlic and honey and heat for 3 minutes.

5. Serve the sausages split in half on a plate, place the cheese on top and then pour over some sauce. Add some more honey if too dry, or some balsamic vinegar.

Courgette Flowers Stuffed with Rabbit Mince, with Red Onion Sauce
Fiori di Zucca Ripieni di Coniglio e Salsa di Cipolla

This beautiful young vegetable is a great gift in spring. In season, courgette flowers are colourful and firm, just like a bunch of flowers. This recipe is an old-fashioned one from my childhood. You can pretty much stuff the flowers with anything you fancy.

Serves 4   Preparation time: 15 minutes   Cooking time: 20 minutes

12 small courgettes with flowers attached
300 g (10½ oz) small courgettes
75 g (2 ¾ oz) shallots, chopped
60 ml (4 tablespoons) extra-virgin olive oil
1 fresh thyme sprig
1 small bunch of fresh Italian parsley, chopped finely
700 g (1 lb 9 oz) rabbit or chicken mince
300 g (10½ oz) well matured tomatoes, diced
2 whole eggs
200 ml (7 fl oz) single cream
salt and freshly ground black pepper to taste

For the sauce:
50 g (1¾ oz) shallots, chopped
1 carrot, chopped
1 celery stick, chopped
butter, for frying
30 ml (2 tablespoons) extra-virgin olive oil
½ teaspoon freshly ground black pepper
leaves of 1 fresh rosemary sprig, chopped
50 ml (2 fl oz) sweet sherry
salt

1. Wash the courgettes with the flowers attached very gently, trying not to break the flowers off. Dry on a piece of kitchen paper. Wash and dry the other courgettes, cut into small cubes and keep to one side.
2. In a frying pan, sauté the shallots with the olive oil, the thyme and the parsley. Now add the mince but reserve two large tablespoons for the sauce.
3. At this point, season and then add the courgettes and tomatoes and continue cooking for 7–8 minutes.
4. In a bowl, beat the eggs with the cream, a pinch of salt and some black pepper. Take the mince off the stove and leave to cool. When cool, add to the eggs and

mix thoroughly, then stuff the flowers one by one, gently twist closed and place on a large platter.

5. In another pan, start making the sauce. Add the shallots, carrot and celery to a little butter and the olive oil and then add the remaining mince, black pepper and herbs and cook for 5 minutes. Add the sherry and a little salt, and reduce over a high heat. Serve the sauce very hot, next to the flowers – and good luck!

Tuna Carpaccio with Shaved Fennel and Parmesan
Carpaccio di Tunno al Finocchio e Scaglie di Parmiggiano

Tuna has to be one of the most versatile fish on the market and nowadays you can find it fresh on fish counters in supermarkets. For this dish you need a really nice loin, not steaks, and a very sharp knife. If you don't want to freeze it then just sear it in a hot pan with olive oil and slice it very thinly.

Serves 4   Preparation time: 15 minutes + 45 minutes freezing

350 g (12 oz) piece of very fresh tuna fillet
200 g (7 oz) fennel bulb
60 ml (4 tablespoons) extra-virgin olive oil
15 ml (1 tablespoon) fresh lemon juice
50 g (1³/₄ oz) parmesan cheese shavings
salt and freshly ground black pepper
lemon wedges and Italian bread, to serve

1. Wrap the tuna in cling film and place in the freezer for 45 minutes; this will make it easier to slice.
2. Use a mandolin to make shavings of the fennel or, if you don't have one, just slice it very thinly.
3. Remove the tuna from the freezer and finely slice into at least 12 slices. Place a slice of tuna between two sheets of cling film and pummel with the base of a saucepan until very thin. Remove from the cling film and place on a plate. Repeat with remaining tuna, placing three pieces on each plate.
4. Put the fennel into a bowl. Add the oil, lemon juice and seasoning and mix well. Pile the fennel on top of the tuna and sprinkle over the parmesan cheese. Serve with lemon wedges and Italian bread.

Field Mushrooms with Goat's Cheese Gratin
Funghi di Bosco Gratinati al Caprino

Serves 4   Preparation time: 15 minutes   Cooking time: 10 minutes

Wild mushroom season is in the autumn and the reason I have chosen to use Portobello mushrooms is because you can find them all year round. My other favourite way of cooking these mushrooms is pan fried with garlic, chilli, olive oil and white wine, and serve it with a really good steak! Tip: don't soak the mushrooms in water.

8 Portobello mushrooms
juice of 1 lemon
30 ml (2 tablespoons) extra-virgin olive oil
1 garlic clove, chopped finely (optional)
8 x 1 cm (½ inch) thick slices of goat's cheese
40 g (1½ oz) freshly grated parmesan cheese
5 ml (1 teaspoon) freshly ground black pepper
balsamic vinegar and olive oil, for drizzling
30 ml (2 tablespoons) chopped fresh flat-leaf parsley

1. Brush the mushrooms clean and remove the stalks. Place the mushrooms on a grill tray, stalk-side up. Squeeze over the lemon and brush with the olive oil. Sprinkle over the garlic and grill for 5 minutes.
2. Place a goat's cheese slice on each mushroom, sprinkle with parmesan and garlic, season and grill for a further 5 minutes or until golden and bubbling. Drizzle with balsamic vinegar and olive oil just before serving and finish with a sprinkle of chopped flat-leaf parsley.

Marisa's Pancake & Chicken Broth
Le Crespelle di mia Cognata

My mom used to feed the whole family with this great dish. She used to make the chicken stock with the whole chicken and then serve the pancake as a starter and the boiled chicken as a main course, with a nice salad. Marisa, my sister-in-law, who I grew up with, still carries on the tradition with this wonderful dish.

Serves 4   Preparation time: 30 minutes   Cooking time: 1 ½ hours

For the stock:

1.5 kg (3 lb 5 oz) chicken

1 celery stick

2 carrots

4 bay leaves

1 onion, studded with cloves

a bunch of fresh flat-leaf parsley

4 garlic cloves

For the pancakes:

4 eggs

300 ml (½ pint) milk

200 g (7 oz) plain flour

30 ml (2 tablespoons) chopped fresh parsley

1 large potato, peeled and cut in half

1 large cup of sunflower oil

salt and freshly ground black pepper

60 ml (4 tablespoons) grated parmesan cheese, to serve

1. You will need a large pan for the stock. Put the chicken in with all the vegetables and herbs. Then cover with water and bring to the boil, reduce the heat and simmer, skimming off the fat with a slotted spoon every so often, for 1 ½ hours.

2. To make the pancakes, whisk the first four ingredients together with a pinch of salt and some pepper, and make sure you don't have any lumps.

3. Heat a non-stick pan or pancake pan until very hot, then insert a fork in the potato half and soak it in the sunflower oil. When the pan is hot enough, rub with the soaked potato and add a small ladle of the pancake mix. Cover the pan and leave until the pancake starts to move. With a spatula, turn the pancake and cook the other side. Continue until you have a stack of pancakes.

4. Strain the stock into a large soup tureen and place in the middle of the table, with a ladle. In four soup bowls, place one pancake or strips of pancakes, pour over the stock and add the parmesan.

5. You can then put the chicken in the middle of the table with a good salad and that is the whole meal.

Italian Apéritifs

What is an apéritif? Well, gone are the days of dry sherry or a gin and tonic. When I arrived in this country the sophistication of apéritif drinking was still going strong. When I opened my first restaurant in the 80s, people still wanted a drink before the meal, but this has slowly fizzled out and nowadays people tend to go straight on to the wine and water. However, the trend in Italy is not only still there but is a whole culture. When you go into a bar in any of the big cities there is a great cocktail like a punch already sitting on the bar and normally they would have alcoholic and non-alcoholic versions. But what is fantastic about it is that they come with a choice of canapés such as mini pizzas, crisps, nuts, olives and mini tramezzini – to name a few – and, if you are not careful, you end up just drinking apéritifs and eating the canapés and not going for your meal. This custom is missing over here, purely due to the licensing laws.

Martini makes a perfect addition to your summer evening: a sophisticated and light drink. For Martini Extra Dry with a twist pour 25 ml (1 fl oz) of **Martini Extra Dry** and 25 ml (1 fl oz) of vodka, add a squeeze of lemon, shake and then serve in a martini glass with an olive and a twist of lemon peel.

Campari is a deep red drink created in Milan which is made from Seville orange peel; this is normally served with fresh orange juice or soda and is a light, refreshing drink for those hot summer days.

Negroni cocktail is gin, Campari, Martini Rosso and soda water, shaken and not stirred, served with a green olive.

ALDO ZILLI

Beef Carpaccio with Rocket, Truffle Oil & Lemon Dressing
Carpaccio di Filetto all'Olio di tartufo, Limone e Rucola

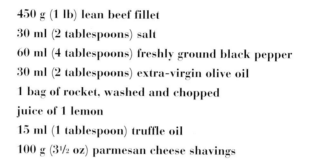

Serves 4   Preparation and cooking time: 5 minutes

Normally you associate carpaccio with raw meat but in my restaurant we also serve fish, such as tuna, salmon or sea-bass, this way. Carpaccio is my favourite way to start a dinner party because you can prepare it beforehand. When you squeeze lemon over and dress the carpaccio with olive oil, the meat or fish starts to change colour, which means it starts 'cooking' a little bit. Just make sure you choose the very best quality meat or fish.

450 g (1 lb) lean beef fillet

30 ml (2 tablespoons) salt

60 ml (4 tablespoons) freshly ground black pepper

30 ml (2 tablespoons) extra-virgin olive oil

1 bag of rocket, washed and chopped

juice of 1 lemon

15 ml (1 tablespoon) truffle oil

100 g (3½ oz) parmesan cheese shavings

1. Season the beef with 15 ml (1 tablespoon) of salt and 30 ml (2 tablespoons) of pepper. Add the extra-virgin olive oil to a frying pan and heat. When very hot, add the beef fillet and sear on all sides (roughly a minute on each side). Allow to cool slightly.

2. Using a sharp, thin-bladed knife, finely slice the beef and arrange on a large plate. Place the rocket on top.

3. Mix the remaining salt and pepper with the lemon juice and truffle oil and drizzle over the rocket and meat. Sprinkle with parmesan shavings and serve.

Grilled Smoked Buffalo Mozzarella Wrapped in Parma Ham
Rotolo di Scamorza al Prosciutto alla Griglia

Suitable for the barbecue. Scamorza is now available in supermarkets; another name for this cheese is smoked mozzarella. It is quite a hard cheese and needs some form of cooking. It is also great in pasta sauces or bakes and is a great party nibble.

Serves: 4   Preparation time: 10 minutes   Cooking time: 20 minutes

2 smoked mozzarellas
8 large slices of parma ham
butter
100 g (3½ oz) parmesan cheese, grated
60 ml (4 tablespoons) olive oil
1 bag of rocket, washed
60 ml (4 tablespoons) balsamic vinegar

1. Cut the mozzarellas into quarters, wrap each quarter with parma ham, and place on a grill tray. Heat the grill to maximum.
2. Place a little butter on each wrap and sprinkle with parmesan and 30 ml (2 tablespoons) of olive oil. Grill for 10–15 minutes or until the mozzarella starts to melt.
3. Get four plates and place some rocket in the centre of each. Arrange the wraps on top of the rocket and sprinkle with the remaining olive oil and the balsamic vinegar. Serve immediately.

Note: If you barbecue, place the wraps on the grill and cook for 5–8 minutes on each side.

Minestra

On Italian farms lunch is made with whatever produce is available at the time. It might be a bean soup made with **chick peas**, **broad beans** and **short pasta**; or it might be a frittata made from the farm's own eggs.

Soups make great meals. One of my favourites has to be a simple bean soup or a great minestrone in which you can use all your **leftover vegetables**. Soups are so simple to make. I don't understand why anyone would buy a ready-made one. I suggest that you invest in a liquidiser and get cooking.

Vegetable and Rice Soup
Minestra di Verdura e Riso

Vegetable soup is always a good idea for warming you up on cold winter evenings. You can, of course, buy soups already made, but I think for the time it takes to make a fresh soup you should make the effort, as the result and taste are so much better than the bought variety. This soup is a classic but you can please yourself as to what you use vegetable-wise and, instead of rice, you could use baby pasta shapes. It is also great to eat it cold in the summer.

Serves 6   Preparation time: 15 minutes   Cooking time: 35 minutes

60 ml (4 tablespoons) extra-virgin olive oil

1 large onion, diced

2 garlic cloves, minced

2 carrots, diced

2 celery sticks, diced

2 courgettes, diced

4 plum tomatoes, skinned, de-seeded and diced

1.2 litres (2 pints) vegetable stock, using 2 stock cubes

500 g (1 lb 2 oz) fresh broad beans, podded,
    or 300 g (10½ oz) frozen broad beans

150 g (5½ oz) long-grain rice

100 g (3½ oz) broccoli, trimmed into florets,
    with stems peeled and chopped

40 g (1½ oz) pecorino romano cheese, grated

salt and freshly ground black pepper

1. In a heavy pan, heat 30 ml (2 tablespoons) of olive oil and stir in the onion. Cook over a low heat for 5 minutes until the onion is soft.

2. Add the garlic and remaining vegetables except for the beans and broccoli florets. Fry for another 5–7 minutes, stirring frequently until all the vegetables look bright in colour.

3. Pour in the stock and bring to the boil. Stir in the beans and rice and season with salt and pepper. Simmer for 10 minutes; the rice should be just al dente.

4. Add the broccoli florets and cook for 5 minutes. Stir in the remaining olive oil and pecorino cheese. Serve with crusty Italian bread.

Vegetarian Flat Omelette
Fritatta Vegetariana

Serves 1   Preparation time: 5 minutes   Cooking time: 10 minutes

You can add pretty much any vegetable or herb to this great egg dish. Make sure that you boil the vegetables until they are soft before you add them to the egg mixture. This has to be the greatest meal you can make when you are on a tight budget. Serve with a crisp salad with olive oil and lemon dressing.

olive oil, for frying
2–3 eggs, beaten
50 g (2 oz) cheese, grated
3 sun-dried tomatoes, chopped
3 olives, stoned and quartered
5 ml (1 teaspoon) chopped fresh parsley
5 ml (1 teaspoon) chopped fresh basil
30 ml (2 tablespoons) milk
salt and freshly ground black pepper

1. Heat the oil in a small non-stick frying pan. Place the rest of the ingredients in a stainless steel bowl and beat.
2. Preheat the grill. Pour the egg mixture into the frying pan and cook over a medium heat for about 5 minutes.
3. Remove the pan from the heat and place under the grill for another 5 minutes or until the top is browned and set.
4. Remove from the heat and place a plate over the top of the pan; flip upside-down and knock the top of the frying pan to get some air underneath; the frittata will then slip out on to the plate, ready for you to cut and serve.

Pasta & Bean Soup
Pasta e Fagioli

I took this recipe from a restaurant I went to in Florence called Latini; it's probably the best winter warmer, but you know what they say about eating too many beans! Good luck.

Serves 4   Preparation time: 5 minutes + overnight soaking
Cooking time: 2 ½ hours

250 g (9 oz) dried cannellini or borlotti beans (or you can use canned)
30 ml (2 tablespoons) extra-virgin olive oil
200 g (7 oz) canned Italian peeled chopped tomatoes
fresh celery leaves
½ onion, chopped
1 garlic clove, chopped finely
fresh basil and parsley, chopped
250 g (9 oz) short pasta

To serve:
grated parmesan cheese
20 ml (2 dessertspoons) extra-virgin olive oil
freshly ground black pepper

1. If using dried beans, soak them overnight
2. After rinsing the beans, cover in water to the depth of three fingers. Cook them, covered, on a moderate heat for 2 hours or until tender. During this time, if you start running out of water just keep adding a little boiling water. Always use a wooden spoon when stirring. When the beans are cooked, drain them.
3. Put the beans in a saucepan, add the oil, tomatoes, celery leaves, onion, garlic and herbs. Cook for 20 minutes on a medium heat with the lid on, stirring occasionally.
4. Meanwhile, cook the pasta according to pack instructions until al dente. Drain well and mix with the beans.
5. Serve with a sprinkling of parmesan, black pepper and a drizzle of extra-virgin olive oil.

Cheeses

We Italians have always loved our cheese. In a recent survey it was revealed that there are 403 different types of cheeses in Italy.

Parmigiano reggiano (parmesan) This is the most famous Italian cheese and has its own certificate to prevent anyone trying to reproduce it. This particular cheese goes back to Roman times. It is produced from cow's milk in precise territorial limits in the region of Emilia Romagna surrounding the cities of Modena, Parma and Reggio Emilia. Having gone through several processes the cheeses are left to mature in large warehouses, under constant care, for a minimum period of 12 months, but the maturing process usually lasts about two years. Every kilogram of parmigiano reggiano is produced with 16 kg of milk!

This is a half-fat, hard cheese which has been cooked before undergoing maturing. It has a gold-coloured crust which is normally 5 mm (¼ in) thick. The actual cheese is a pale yellow colour with a delicate and pungent taste. It is mainly served freshly grated but is also good with pears, nuts or grapes as an after-dinner snack.

Grana padano also has its own certificate and is made from cow's milk. It is a hard, half-fat cheese that has gone through a slow maturation process. The crust is pale yellow, hard and smooth. The cheese itself is pale yellow and granular in consistency (hence its name). Grana padano is suitable for appetisers, served in little slivers accompanied by a white wine. It also goes really well with raw vegetables such as lettuce, artichokes, celery and mushrooms and is brilliant when served with carpaccio.

Pecorino romano is produced from sheep's milk and is considered to be one of the oldest cheeses in the world. During the reign of Emperor Augustus a daily ration of 30 g (about 1 oz) was sent to soldiers. Pecorino is still salted according to the ancient complicated technique, demanding high levels of craftsmanship. The cheese can be sold after five months of maturing for eating at the table and after eight months if used for grating. It is a hard, cooked cheese which is cylindrical in shape, with the crust being ivory white or pale yellow, although sometimes it is covered with a neutral or black protective substance. The cheese itself is white or very pale yellow with a strong, fragrant perfume and a light spicy taste.

Gorgonzola is one of the best-known cow's milk cheeses and is made in the town of Gorgonzola, not far from Milan, where it began to be produced over a thousand years ago. It is a soft cheese with a rough texture. The colour of the cheese is white or pale yellow streaked through with green, with a hard crust and a slightly spicy flavour. As a table cheese it is a speciality and is used in numerous sauces. It is best to buy Gorgonzola in small quantities as it is considered a live food product which is still maturing. The best way to keep Gorgonzola is wrapped in tinfoil in the lower half of the fridge. Before eating, however, you must keep it at room temperature for at least half an hour so that the flavour can be restored.

Taleggio takes its name from an alpine valley, the Val Taleggio near Bergamo. It is produced entirely from cow's milk which is usually pasteurised and matured over a period of 2530 days. This is a soft cheese with a rough, thin, light-brown crust. The cheese itself is compact with a few small holes, slightly softer than the crust, with a white or pale yellow colour. It has an aromatic perfume and a sweet, delicate and slightly spicy flavour. Taleggio is mainly used as a table cheese and you will see that I have fried the cheese to make a salad (see page 44); gorgeous!

Everyone knows what **mozzarella** is, as it is easily available in most supermarkets. The best is the buffalo-milk mozzarella, mozzarella di bufala, which is entirely made from the milk of water buffalo reared in the marshlands of the Campania and Latium regions. This cheese is made by the coagulation of milk induced by natural lactic fermentation; after a period of 5 hours the curd is placed in tanks containing water at a temperature of 95°C where it is stretched and broken up into portions. After this the cheese is immersed in cold water for a few minutes and then salted for a short while in brine, before it is wrapped up and ready to be eaten. Mozzarella is always packed floating in its own whey to keep it moist. It should be eaten within 15 days, and it should always be left out for at least an hour before eating to get the best flavour. The other mozzarella available is made from cow's milk and is manufactured in the same way but does not have the same flavour. It is best to use this mozzarella when cooking. You can tell the difference between the two by looking at the packing: buffalo mozzarella has a circled stylised buffalo head on the packet.

Asiago is obtained from the milk of cows that have been fed on meadow fodder and mountain pasture. There are two types. Aisago d'allevo is a half-fat cheese with scattered small or average-sized holes; it is yellow or pale yellow and has a fragrant taste. The other is Asiago pressato, which is a full-fat cheese that is only half cooked. It has well defined, irregularly scattered holes, and it is white or creamy white with a sweet, delicate taste.

Mascarpone is obtained from the cream of cow's or buffalo milk. It is a fresh cheese which is soft and creamy with a lovely delicate flavour and is widely known due to the fact that it is one of the main ingredients of tiramisù.

Ricotta is produced from either cow's or sheep's milk. The sweet ricotta is snow white in colour and soft and finely granulated, and it is best for stuffing ravioli. The harder salty ricotta has been salted and dried before packing and is good in salads.

Salads

We Italians eat a lot of salads. One of my favourites has to be **radicchio** and fennel with parmesan. **Rocket** has become one of the most popular salad leaves; if you manage to find the wild variety, which tastes a bit peppery, you will realise why. When I was a kid my mother would get us to pick wild salad leaves and then she would mix them up and dress them with some extra-virgin olive oil and lemon – **fantastic stuff**.

Four-Bean Salad
Insalata Quattro Fagioli

This is a great starter or main course for a nice light spring or summer dish. It is very important that you use good quality beans. I love french green beans and now you can also get the white variety. Remember in salad there are no rules so add or take away whatever you think you might like or not enjoy.

Serves 4

Preparation time: 10 minutes + overnight soaking + 30 minutes chilling

400 g (14 oz) fresh or canned borlotti beans

400 g (14 oz) white french beans

400 g (14 oz) broad beans

400 g (14 oz) french beans

1 red onion, chopped finely

3 tomatoes, chopped

2 celery sticks, chopped

99 g can of tuna, drained

For the dressing:

90 ml (scant 4 fl oz) extra-virgin olive oil

30 ml (2 tablespoons) white wine vinegar

1 garlic clove, crushed

5 ml (1 teaspoon) Dijon mustard

salt and freshly ground black pepper

1. If using fresh borlotti beans they must be soaked overnight, and washed thoroughly and then cooked.
2. All the other beans need to be cooked, but left al dente, just a little crunchy, and then plunged into cold water and drained.
3. Empty the cans of beans into a colander, rinse under cold water and drain well.
4. Put the beans in a large bowl and then add the onion, tomatoes, celery and tuna and mix well.
5. Place the ingredients for the dressing in a bowl and mix well using a whisk.
6. Pour the dressing over the bean mixture and stir gently but thoroughly. Season to taste and refrigerate for at least an hour before serving.

Trevisano Radicchio, Fennel & Parmesan Salad
Trevisano, Finocchio e Parmigiano

Serves 4   Preparation time: 10 minutes

Treviso is where this type of radicchio comes from and it is a different shape from your normal one: it looks more like endive only red in colour. It is full of flavour and is also good in risottos – in fact all of these ingredients would make a nice risotto. This has to be the simplest and tastiest recipe for salad.

2 heads of Trevisano radicchio, torn
2 bulbs of fennel, sliced
50 g (1³/₄ oz) parmesan cheese, shaved

For the dressing:
2 garlic cloves, crushed
5 ml (1 teaspoon) English mustard
30 ml (2 tablespoons) olive oil
15 ml (1 tablespoon) white wine vinegar
15 ml (1 tablespoon) chopped fresh parsley

1. In a small bowl, whisk together the garlic, mustard, olive oil and vinegar and then stir in the parsley.
2. In a large bowl, toss the radicchio and fennel together, drizzle with dressing and serve with parmesan shavings on top.

Fried Taleggio, Tomato & Basil Salad
Fritto di Taleggio, Pomodoro e Basilico

Taleggio cheese is very underrated in this country. I love this cheese – it tastes a bit like Brie only better (well, I think so, anyway). It's great to grill on top of some vegetables or in pasta sauces but I have chosen one of my mother's recipes because it reminds me of growing up.

Serves 4   Preparation time: 10 minutes + chilling

Cooking time: 5 minutes

300 g (10½ oz) Taleggio cheese with rind

1 egg

15 ml (1 tablespoon) flour, mixed with 45 ml (3 tablespoons)
   of breadcrumbs, for coating cheese

4 plum tomatoes, sliced

1 red onion, sliced

20 g (scant 1 oz) fresh basil leaves

olive oil, for deep-frying

15 ml (1 tablespoon) basil oil (available from delicatessens,
   or see page 47), to serve

salt and freshly ground black pepper

1. Cut the Taleggio into 2 cm (¾ in) cubes, and then put back into the refrigerator to chill. If not chilled well the cheese will melt too quickly when being fried.

2. Beat the egg with 30 ml (2 tablespoons) of cold water and place in a dish. Place a few of the cubes at a time in the egg mixture and then roll in the mixture of flour and breadcrumbs, to coat fully.

3. Mix the tomatoes, red onion and basil and arrange on four plates.

4. Deep-fry the Taleggio quickly in the olive oil until golden. Serve on top of the salad and drizzle with basil oil. Season to taste. Serve immediately.

Italian Vinegar

Balsamic vinegar originated in the region of Emilia Romagna in the cities of Modena and Reggio Emilia, where the marked changes in temperature from summer to winter and day to night make balsamic vinegar possible. Balsamic vinegar is obtained through a long, slow process of transformation, starting from the concentrated grape must. This transformation takes place in barrels which are stored in attics, so that they can be exposed to the most extreme temperatures changes. The whole process is extremely slow and can go on for decades!

The two main types of vinegar are **traditional balsamic vinegar of Modena** and **traditional balsamic vinegar of Reggio Emilia**. They are described as 'traditional' because they are produced according to similar ancient regulations that have been passed on by word of mouth from father to son. The grape must is concentrated over an open flame until reduced by half and is then left to decant until the spring, when it is poured into barrels and stored in the attic. The production cycle consists of the gradual evaporation and decanting of the liquid from one barrel to another. The ageing process is spread over a required number of years, usually 12. If the process lasts more than 25 years it becomes extra vecchio, meaning 'extra old'. Traditional balsamic has an intense dark colour with a syrupy consistency.

The rule when using balsamic vinegar in cooking is that less is more; too much balsamic will overpower any dish. A great money-saving idea is to buy a basic balsamic vinegar, decant it into a pan and reduce the liquid by half. You end up with a sweeter flavoured vinegar that is perfect for dressing fruit and salads.

Wine vinegar is derived simply from the fermentation of alcohol within the grape, and is easily obtainable and great for making your own infusions, such as raspberry vinegar. The method for this is quite simple: decant into a pan and bring to the boil, add as many raspberries as you wish (the more you add the stronger the flavour), switch off the heat and leave to cool. When cool strain the liquid so that you are left with a red, clear vinegar which is fantastic with salads and fish. You can also make herb vinegar, such as tarragon.

Italian Olive Oil

Just in the last year or so I have been exploring Italy, with a view to expanding my knowledge of organic ingredients and olive oils – purely because I have a deli now.

Olio Carli, which comes from Liguria right up in the north of Italy. This oil is low in acidity and is good for salads.

Ravida is from Sicily, which is a fantastic island for food and wine in general, but its award-winning Ravida extra-virgin has to be one of the best olive oils it has produced. It is a blend of three organically grown olive varieties.

Filippo Cassetta from Puglia has a great flavour and is the best olive oil you could use when making a tomato sauce for your pasta.

Vestino, from Abruzzo, is a great choice of extra-virgin olive oil and is bottled by the producer himself. It is slightly thinner than the others but retains its flavour.

Il Cardinale, from the Puglia region, is ideal for salad dressings and for finishing grilled dishes such as fish and chicken. This oil has not been filtered and is therefore quite intense so use it with care; less is more.

The best olive oil is unrefined olive oil which is separated into two grades, 'extra-virgin' and 'virgin', according to its acidity. The lower the acidity, the better the oil. Extra-virgin oil tends to have an acidity level no higher than 1% whereas virgin olive oil has an acidity level no higher than 2%.

Flavouring olive oils is becoming more and more popular and I am a big fan of doing it yourself rather than spending a lot of money on bought flavoured oils. The method is as follows, should you wish to make garlic oil the best way is to put whole, peeled garlic cloves in a pan with the olive oil (amounts will vary but, as a guide, for 1 litre /1¾ pints of oil you will need 8 cloves). Bring the oil up to boiling point but do not boil, remove from the heat and leave to cool. Then decant into a bottle which has a cork (leave the cloves in the bottle as this will continue flavouring the oil). Keep out of the sunlight and store in a cool place. This process is the same for herbs. You can, of course, get creative and start making combinations like garlic, chilli and lemon oil. The more you make your own oils, the better you will get at it.

Root Vegetable Salad
Verdure e Insalata

Most root vegetables can be eaten raw and if you like them it is a great way to have a healthy snack. I love keeping in the fridge lots of different vegetables to snack on, especially if I am on a diet! In this recipe I cook them a little just to soften them, but it is up to you to do what you fancy.

Serves 4   Preparation time: 10 minutes   Cooking time: 15 minutes

2 large carrots

1 small celeriac

1 large potato

4 garlic cloves, chopped finely

25 g (1 oz) fresh rosemary leaves, chopped roughly

25 g (1 oz) fresh basil leaves, chopped roughly

300 ml (½ pint) extra-virgin olive oil

juice of 2 lemons

1 small cauliflower, cut in small florets

1 head of broccoli, cut in small florets

1 bulb of fennel, sliced very thinly

2 celery sticks, sliced

200 g (7 oz) rocket

salt and freshly ground black pepper

45 ml (3 tablespoons) balsamic vinegar, to serve

1. Preheat the oven to 180°C/fan oven 160°C/Gas Mark 4.
2. Wash and peel the carrots, celeriac and potatoes and chop them into uniform 1 cm (½-inch) cubes. Place on a baking tray and sprinkle with the garlic.
3. Sprinkle half the rosemary and basil over the vegetables.
4. Pour over the olive oil and lemon juice and generously season with salt and pepper. Place in the oven until all the vegetables are soft and cooked.
5. Remove the vegetables from the oven and allow to cool.
6. Put the vegetables into a large bowl and sprinkle with the remainder of the basil and rosemary.
7. Add the cauliflower and broccoli florets, fennel, celery and rocket leaves. Shake to mix fully. Check the seasoning.
8. Drizzle the balsamic vinegar over just before serving.

Seafood Salad
Insalata di Mare

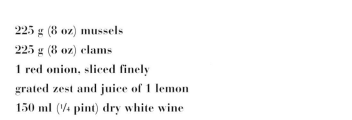

I recommend several different kinds of fish in this recipe but you can pretty much please yourself and use what is available when you make it. Nowadays it is not very easy to find a good fishmonger, so try to order in advance.

Serves 4   Preparation time: 35 minutes + 30 minutes soaking
Cooking time: 10 minutes

225 g (8 oz) mussels
225 g (8 oz) clams
1 red onion, sliced finely
grated zest and juice of 1 lemon
150 ml (¼ pint) dry white wine
175 g (6 oz) firm fish fillet, e.g. cod, salmon or haddock,
    skinned and cut in 2 cm (¾ inch) pieces
4 raw king prawns, peeled and de-veined
225 g (8 oz) squid, cleaned and cut in rings
125 g (4½ oz) peeled prawns
2 x 415 g cans cannellini beans, drained, rinsed
    and patted dry with kitchen paper
1 red pepper, de-seeded and sliced finely
1 yellow pepper, de-seeded and sliced finely

For the dressing:
100 ml (3½ oz) extra-virgin olive oil
30 ml (2 tablespoons) red wine vinegar
45 ml (3 tablespoons) chopped fresh flat-leaf parsley
1 garlic clove, diced finely
salt and freshly ground black pepper

1. Scrub the mussels clean and remove the beards and barnacles. Soak the clams in salted water for 30 minutes to remove the grit, and then wash in clean water and drain.
2. Put the onion in a large non-metallic bowl and stir in the lemon zest and juice; this will keep the onion red and crisp.
3. Pour the wine into a deep heavy-based pan with a steamer basket. Place the fish fillet, mussels, clams and king prawns in the basket and put in the pan. Cover tightly and cook for 5 minutes, shaking the pan once. The shellfish are cooked once the shells have opened; discard any that have remained closed. The king prawns are cooked when they change colour to pink. The fish should be tender and just beginning to flake. Using a slotted spoon, remove the fish and shellfish and transfer to a large plate. Set aside.

4. Add the squid and peeled prawns to the pan juices and cook for 1–2 minutes until tender. Using a slotted spoon, drain and transfer to the plate with the mussels and clams. Bring the pan juices to the boil and cook for 2–3 minutes until reduced to 4 tablespoons.

5. Mix the cannellini beans with the onion, then stir in the red and yellow peppers and all the fish and shellfish.

6. In a small bowl, mix together the oil, vinegar, parsley, garlic and reserved pan juices. Season well to taste. Pour the dressing over the salad mixture and toss gently. Serve with crusty bread.

Baby Spinach, Pancetta & Mushroom Salad
Spinaci, Funghi e Pancetta

It is very important in this recipe that you make the pancetta nice and crisp. If you can't find pancetta then smoked bacon will do, but make an effort to find the right ingredients for this one as it will make a big difference to the end result.

Serves 4   Preparation time: 10 minutes   Cooking time: 15 minutes

500 g (1 lb 2 oz) new potatoes, halved

75 g (2³/₄ oz) green beans, topped and tailed

225 g (8 oz) pancetta, cut in 1 cm (¹/₂ in) cubes
   (or you can buy the pancetta in cubes)

225 g (8 oz) baby spinach

300 g (10¹/₂ oz) cherry tomatoes, halved

100 g (4 oz) button mushrooms, sliced

For the dressing:

30 ml (2 tablespoons) Italian honey

15 ml (1 tablespoon) wholegrain mustard

30 ml (2 tablespoons) crème fraîche

1. Boil the potatoes for 15 minutes or until just cooked, then drain. Meanwhile, boil the green beans for 3 minutes until tender but still crunchy. Drain and plunge into iced water. Drain thoroughly.

2. Preheat the grill, place the pancetta under the heat and cook for 4–6 minutes, turning occasionally until the pancetta is crisp. Put on to kitchen paper and pat dry.

3. In a large salad bowl, put the potatoes, green beans, pancetta, spinach, tomatoes and mushrooms.

4. Mix together the ingredients for the dressing and pour over the salad. Toss and serve immediately.

Goat's Cheese Salad with Rocket, Baked Plum Tomatoes & Sauteéd Pears
Formaggio di Capra, Pera e Pomodoro Arrosto

This has to be one of my favourite ways of serving tomatoes. Make sure you use a good goat's cheese. The pears must be quite hard, which is not that difficult as most supermarkets sell them that way.

Serves 4   Preparation time: 10 minutes   Cooking time: 18 minutes

4 plum tomatoes
45 ml (3 tablespoons) olive oil
8 slices of goat's cheese
4 firm pears, peeled and sliced
5 ml (1 teaspoon) white sugar
50 g (1³/₄ oz) butter
125 g (4¹/₂ oz) rocket
15 ml (1 tablespoon) good balsamic vinegar, to serve
salt and freshly ground black pepper

1. Preheat the grill.
2. Slice the tomatoes in half and place on a tray, drizzle with a tablespoon of olive oil and grill for 10 minutes, until soft but still firm. Place a slice of goat's cheese on each tomato half, and set aside.
3. Sprinkle the pears with the sugar and pan-fry in the butter until soft (add more butter if you need).
4. Place the tomato and goat's cheese under the grill and cook until the top of the goat's cheese is a light golden colour.
5. Serve the tomato and goat's cheese on top of the rocket with the sautéed pear on the side. Drizzle with the remaining olive oil and balsamic vinegar and season to taste.

Rice Salad
Insalata di Riso

Risotto has to be my favourite dish to cook but, in the summer, I love cold rice and made this way it will be full of flavour. My way of making this salad is really simple: just make sure you don't overcook the rice, otherwise, you will end up with a sticky mess!

Serves 4   Preparation time: 15 minutes

125 g (4½ oz) Arborio rice

15 ml (1 tablespoon) lemon juice

60 ml (4 tablespoons) olive oil

10 ml (2 teaspoons)
    snipped fresh chives

10 ml (2 teaspoons)
    chopped fresh parsley

10 ml (2 teaspoons)
    chopped fresh tarragon

10 ml (2 teaspoons)
    chopped fresh basil

150 g (5½ oz) ricotta cheese

75 g (2¾ oz) fresh peas, blanched

½ large cucumber, peeled,
    sliced and quartered

326 g can of sweetcorn, drained

salt and freshly ground
    black pepper

1. Wash the rice and cook until tender, then drain. Lay out on a tray to cool and dry.

2. When cool, put the rice into a large bowl, add the rest of the ingredients and season to taste.

Borlotti Bean & Provolone Salad
Fagioli Provolone e Prezzemolo

When you go and look for provolone, make sure you find the piccante (spicy) variety; it will make a difference to the taste of this great salad. As the cheese is quite spicy, watch the black pepper on this one.

Serves 4   Preparation time: 15 minutes

45 ml (3 tablespoons) olive oil
30 ml (2 tablespoons) tapenade
2 x 400 g cans of borlotti beans,
    drained and rinsed
5 plum tomatoes, halved
1 small red onion, sliced finely

1 garlic clove, sliced thinly
200 g (7 oz) provolone, cut in cubes
salt and freshly ground
    black pepper
fresh basil leaves, to garnish
extra-virgin olive oil, to serve

1. Mix the olive oil and the tapenade and then add the borlotti beans and mix so that the beans are coated in the tapenade.

2. Add the tomatoes, red onion, garlic and provolone to the bean mixture and toss.

3. Season the salad. Divide into four servings and scatter some basil leaves on top. Serve immediately, drizzled with olive oil.

Capers & Olives

The variety of olives available in the UK is much bigger than it used to be but my favourite is still the familiar stoned black olives, which I dress myself with olive oil, chilli, sun-dried tomatoes, salt, pepper and coriander. You will find the taste is much better than that of the olives you buy that have already been marinated and they will also be a lot cheaper. On our family farm we had an olive tree, so there was never a problem with getting olives, but my family tended not to marinate them because my father would press his own olive oil to sell to the local shops; any olive oil we had was strictly for sale and not for extras
like marinating.

Olives that have just been picked are very bitter and inedible; it is the salt-curing process that makes them edible. When picked the olives are green (unripe) and they then undergo a curing process. By the time you buy them they are preserved in brine (salt water) and can range in colour from green to deep violet and black. The interesting thing is that the olives you eat are usually completely different from the olives used to make olive oil. Italian markets sell a huge range of olives, sometimes more than 20 different varieties, whole and stuffed. Most are eaten in antipasti but some are only suitable for cooking.

Capers are wild plants that grow all over the place and originated from Asia and Africa before moving over to the Mediterranean. The plants, especially the roots and branches, had therapeutic properties but these days they are no longer recognised as healing plants. The caper is actually the bud of a fairly large plant, and the smaller they are, the stronger the flavour. Like olives, capers are bitter when first picked and they need to be cured in either vinegar or brine.

The most common capers are the very little ones, which are a vital ingredient in tartare sauce or a green pickle sauce for boiled meat. My favourites are caper berries, which are still on the stalks and can be eaten like olives and dressed in the same way.

ALDO ZILLI

Baby Spinach, Figs, Pears, Walnuts & Balsamic Salad
Fichi, Pera, Spinaci, Noci e Balsamico

All of these ingredients are fantastic. The only drawback about this salad is that using figs when they are not in season means that they don't have a lot of flavour. We used to have a fig tree in our garden so as kids we picked all our figs in September – what a joy! Now I have to rely on supermarkets to bring them in, so perhaps it is best that you make this salad in the autumn.

Serves 4   Preparation time: 10 minutes

225 g (8 oz) baby spinach leaves
125 g (4½ oz) quartered ripe figs
1 ripe pear, peeled and cut in
    1 cm (½ inch) cubes
50 g (1¾ oz) walnuts
15 ml (1 tablespoon) freshly
    squeezed lemon juice

45 ml (3 tablespoons) extra-virgin
    olive oil
salt and freshly ground
    black pepper
45 ml (3 tablespoons) good,
    thick balsamic vinegar, to serve

1. Wash the baby spinach well, tear into pieces and dry well.
2. Add the quartered figs, diced pear and walnuts.
3. In a small bowl, mix the lemon juice with the olive oil and pour on to the salad, mixing thoroughly to coat everything.
4. Season to taste with salt and pepper and arrange on a plate. Drizzle with balsamic vinegar and serve immediately.

Pasta Salad
Insalata di Penne

I have used penne for this recipe, but you can take your pick, as any dried pasta will do (only I would not use spaghetti). Try to stick with short pasta. Make this recipe because it is great to keep for a few days and, if you fancy, add some chilli and garlic for that extra kick.

Serves 4   Preparation time: 10 minutes   Cooking time: 10 minutes

250 g (9 oz) penne
30 ml (2 tablespoons) extra-virgin
    olive oil
8 cherry tomatoes, cut in quarters
150 g (5½ oz) tub boccancini di
    mozzarella (baby mozzarella
    balls), quartered
15 g (½ oz) fresh basil, chopped
1 small can of sweetcorn, drained

1 red onion, sliced finely
3 radicchio leaves, sliced
100 g (3½ oz) stoned black
    and green olives
30 ml (2 tablespoons) sun-dried
    tomato purée
salt and freshly ground
    black pepper

1. Cook the pasta al dente, according to the pack instructions. Then drain, drizzle with olive oil, shake to cover fully, and allow to cool completely.
2. When cool, place the penne in a large bowl, add all the other ingredients and mix together well. Season to taste.

Pasta

I could talk to you about pasta forever, but then you would end up bored, so I am just going to give you a few tips. When buying and cooking pasta, you can use **dried** or **fresh**, but make sure the brand you buy is a good Italian brand. There are lots of them, but my favourite is Buitoni. Cook the pasta for 7 to 8 minutes and finish cooking it in the sauce. Or if you are not using it straightaway, drain it and cool it down with some oil.

Spaghetti with Olive Oil, Garlic & Chilli
Spaghetti, Aglio Olio, e Peperoncino

Serves 4   Preparation time: 5 minutes   Cooking time: 15 minutes

In my family this recipe was always a quickie solution when my mother didn't have enough time to make a sauce or she had to go to work in the fields. If you are giving it to children you could omit the chilli, but we never did and I love chilli now, so you could start as you mean to go on!!

60 ml (4 tablespoons) good olive oil

3 garlic cloves, crushed

2 fresh red chillies, de-seeded and chopped finely

400 g (14 oz) spaghetti

100 g (3½ oz) parmesan cheese, grated

10 fresh basil leaves, torn

1 tablespoon chopped fresh flat-leaf parsley

1. Heat the oil in a pan, add the garlic and chillies and sauté for about 3 minutes until the garlic is soft; make sure that you cook over a medium heat as you do not want to burn the garlic. If you wish, at this point you could discard the garlic because the olive oil will already have been infused with its flavour.
2. Cook the spaghetti according to pack instructions and drain thoroughly.
3. Add the pasta and parmesan to the pan with a little of the water from the pasta pot and toss to combine. Serve immediately with a sprinkling of fresh basil and parsley.

Lasagne

Serves 6   Preparation time: 10 minutes   Cooking time: 1 ½ hours

This classic dish is always a winner in any household. I remember my sister never used to chop the vegetables at all and she would take them out just before assembling the lasagne as they would have already left their flavour in the sauce. The same applies to the herbs: I recommend a bouquet garni, to be taken out at the end.

30 ml (2 tablespoons) olive oil
1 large onion, chopped finely
1 small carrot, chopped finely
1 celery stick, chopped
2 garlic cloves, crushed
½ teaspoon ground cinnamon
350 g (12 oz) minced pork or beef
125 ml (4 fl oz) good red wine
15 ml (1 tablespoon) tomato purée
5 ml (1 teaspoon) chopped fresh oregano
5 ml (1 teaspoon) chopped fresh parsley
200 g (7 oz) canned tomatoes
300 ml (½ pint) beef stock
salt and freshly ground black pepper

For the lasagne:
300 ml (½ pint) béchamel sauce (see page 76)
6 no-pre-cook lasagne sheets
25 g (1 oz) parmesan cheese, grated
25 g (1 oz) pecorino cheese, grated

1. Preheat the oven to 190°C/fan oven 170°C/Gas Mark 5.
2. Heat the oil in a saucepan and cook the onion, carrot and celery over a low heat for about 10–12 minutes or until the onion is soft. Add the garlic and cinnamon and carry on cooking for 2 minutes. Then add the mince and cook over a medium heat, breaking the mince up with a fork.
3. Once all the meat is browned and all the juices have evaporated, add the red wine. Cook until the wine has completely evaporated.
4. Add the rest of the ingredients, bring to the boil and simmer over a low heat for about 45 minutes, stirring frequently.
5. Skim away any fat from the sauce and bring back to the boil to reduce any excess liquid. Season to taste.
6. Take an ovenproof pie dish and begin assembling the lasagne. Start by spooning some of the meat sauce on to the bottom. Then place a layer of pasta on top and cover with béchamel sauce. Carry on until the dish is full, finishing with a layer of sauce.

7. Sprinkle the top with the cheese, place on a baking tray and bake in the oven for 25–30 minutes or until the top is brown and crisp and the pasta is tender. Serve with a mixed leaf salad.

Spaghetti Bolognese My Way

There are many different ways of making this great sauce but pork mince is one of my favourites and, if you can find Italian sausages, the end product will have a lot more flavour. Also, pecorino cheese is quite a bit stronger and more peppery than parmesan and it will make a difference to the overall taste. Remember this is just a guideline; if you like beef mince and parmesan use them; you are, after all, the one eating the dish!

Serves 4   Preparation time: 10 minutes
Cooking time: 1 hour 20 minutes

350 g (12 oz) spaghetti
60 ml (4 tablespoons) pecorino or parmesan cheese, grated

For the sauce:
8 fresh Italian pork and garlic sausages
15 ml (1 tablespoon) olive oil
1 onion, chopped finely
2 carrots, chopped finely
1 celery stick, chopped finely
225 ml (8 fl oz) vegetable stock
2 flat mushrooms, chopped
2 glasses of good red wine
2 fresh thyme sprigs, tough stalks removed
800 g (1¾ lb) canned Italian plum tomatoes or 1 jar passata
salt and freshly ground black pepper

1. Preheat the oven to 200°C/fan oven 180°C/Gas Mark 6. Place the sausages on a baking tray and cook in the oven for 10 minutes.

2. Heat the oil in a large saucepan, add the onion, carrots and celery and pour in the stock. Cook for 5 minutes. Chop the sausage and add to the pan together with the chopped mushrooms and red wine. Cook for a further 5 minutes or until the wine has evaporated. Stir in the thyme leaves and tomatoes (or passata) with their juice. Season with salt and freshly ground black pepper. Cover and cook for 1 hour until the sauce is thick, stirring occasionally.

3. During the final 10 minutes of the sauce's cooking time, cook the pasta in a large pan of boiling, salted water for 5–8 minutes, or according to the instructions on the packet, until al dente. Drain and transfer to a large pasta bowl. Pour the sauce over the pasta. Sprinkle with the cheese and toss to mix. Serve immediately.

Pappardelle with Tuna Meatballs
Polpettine di Tonno e Pappardella

Serves 4   Cooking time: 10 minutes   Preparation time: 30 minutes

Meatballs are normally associated with meat, but tuna does remind me of beef and it is quite a firm fish so it can be treated in the same way. If you don't fancy pasta, then just make a nice tomato sauce and serve the tuna balls as a starter or main course with salad.

400 g (14 oz) pappardelle
salt and freshly ground black pepper
chopped fresh flat-leaf parsley, to garnish

For the tuna meatballs:
500 g (1 lb 2 oz) fresh tuna, chopped finely, fat and sinew removed
4 spring onions, chopped finely
2 garlic cloves, chopped finely
2 large shallots, chopped finely
2 long red chillies, de-seeded and chopped finely
5 ml (1 teaspoon) dried oregano
30 ml (2 tablespoons) finely chopped fresh parsley
5 ml (1 teaspoon) finely chopped fresh coriander
5 ml (1 teaspoon) finely chopped fresh basil
2 egg yolks
100 g (3½ oz) fine breadcrumbs
100 ml (3½ fl oz) olive oil

For the sauce:
15 ml (1 tablespoon) extra-virgin olive oil
1 onion, chopped finely
1 garlic clove, chopped finely
1 large jar of passata

1. Mix the tuna with the spring onions, garlic, shallots, chillies and herbs. Season and then add the egg yolks and half the breadcrumbs. Roll into small balls and then roll in the remaining breadcrumbs until they are completely coated. Pan-fry in the olive oil for about 3–4 minutes until golden.

2. Make the tomato sauce. Heat the oil in a frying pan, add the onion and garlic and cook for 3 minutes until soft but not brown, then add the jar of passata and simmer for 10 minutes. Then add the tuna balls and cook for a further 4 minutes.

3. Meanwhile, cook the pappardelle according to pack instructions. Drain well and add to the tuna ball sauce. Season and serve immediately with a sprinkling of parsley (making sure everyone gets enough tuna balls).

Penne with Spicy Tomato Sauce
Penne Arrabbiata

Another Italian classic, but too many Italian restaurants use canned tomatoes for tomato sauce; for this recipe fresh tomatoes in season are unbeatable, so make the most of them.

Serves 4   Preparation time: 10 minutes   Cooking time: 35 minutes

60 ml (4 tablespoons) olive oil

1 small onion, chopped finely

2 fresh chillies, de-seeded and sliced

1 garlic clove, crushed

450 g (1 lb) cherry tomatoes

15 g (½ oz) basil, torn into small pieces

5 ml (1 teaspoon) soft brown sugar (optional)

400 g (14 oz) penne

½ vegetable stock cube (optional)

salt and freshly ground black pepper

60 g (2 oz) parmesan cheese, grated, to serve

1. Heat the oil in a large, deep frying pan; add the onion and chillies and cook over a very low heat for about 5 minutes, until the onion is soft but not brown.

2. Stir in the garlic, tomatoes and basil. Cook over a low heat for 10 minutes; the tomatoes will soften so mash gently with the back of a wooden spoon. Continue to simmer for another 20 minutes until the sauce is very thick.

3. Season with salt and freshly ground black pepper to taste, adding a little sugar if needed to balance the acidity of the tomatoes.

4. Meanwhile, bring a large pan of salted water to a rolling boil. Add the penne, gently easing it into the water. Return to a gentle rolling boil and cook for 10–12 minutes until al dente. Remember to stir the pasta occasionally.

5. Drain the pasta, reserving about 100 ml (3 ½ fl oz) of the cooking water. Mix the stock cube in the reserved water. Toss the penne into the sauce and combine well, adding as much of the reserved water as needed to loosen the pasta and sauce. Serve immediately with the parmesan sprinkled on top.

Trenette al Pesto

In Italy we use different pasta for different sauces and this has to be the most classic combination. It brings back memories of when I worked the summer season in hotels in the Costa Ligure near Genova, which is where pesto comes from. Pesto is also fantastic for dressing grilled fish. You could change the trenette to gnocchi and get the same result a – really lovely light dish for the summer months.

Serves 4   Preparation time: 10 minutes   Cooking time: 10 minutes

400 g (14 oz) trenette pasta

For the pesto:
200 g (7 oz) fresh basil
2 garlic cloves
25 g (1 oz) pine nuts
50 g (1¾ oz) parmesan cheese, grated
50 g (1¾ oz) pecorino sweet sardo, grated
100 ml (3½ fl oz) extra-virgin olive oil
100 g (3½ oz) green beans (retain 8 beans for decoration)
2 small potatoes, par-boiled
salt and freshly ground black pepper

1. Clean the basil leaves with a damp cloth and place in a pestle and mortar or food processor. Add the garlic, pine nuts and some salt and pepper and start slowly working the ingredients together.
2. Then add the cheeses, olive oil, beans and potatoes. Carry on grinding until you achieve a paste.
3. Top and tail the 8 beans for decoration and cook in boiling, salted water until just cooked but still crunchy.
4. In a large pot, boil the salted water for the pasta and cook until al dente, then drain.
5. Add the pasta to the sauce and mix together. Return to the pan and heat quickly. Serve immediately, topped with the reserved beans.

PECORINO
di CAMPAGNA

Fettuccine with Lamb Ragout & Pecorino
Fettuccine Ragu d'Agnello

Lamb is quite an unusual meat to make a pasta sauce with, but in my lovely home region this is a signature dish. It's a little on the heavy side but nevertheless you must go for this; it is one of my favourite recipes in this book.

Serves 6   Preparation time: 20 minutes + 1 hour marinating   Cooking time: 2–2 ½ hours

1 lamb shoulder weighing about 2.4 kg (5½ lb) unboned weight, or a leg of lamb, boned, bones reserved
200 ml (7 fl oz) good white wine
60 ml (4 tablespoons) olive oil
3 white spanish onions, sliced
2 garlic cloves, chopped
2 celery sticks, chopped
200 ml (7 fl oz) meat or vegetable stock
leaves of 2 fresh thyme sprigs
2 bay leaves
leaves of 2 fresh rosemary sprigs
900 g (2 lb) canned chopped Italian plum tomatoes
500 g (1 lb 2 oz) fettuccine
200 g (7 oz) pecorino cheese, grated, to serve

1. Cut the lamb into small cubes and marinate in the wine for approximately 1 hour.
2. Preheat the oven to 200°C/fan oven 180°C/Gas Mark 6 and put the lamb bones in to roast for about 30 minutes, until golden brown.
3. Brown the lamb in the olive oil in a large frying pan at a high heat.
4. In the same pan, gently brown the onions, garlic and celery. Place the browned bones in a casserole pot or large pan. Pour the wine that the lamb had been marinating in on to the vegetables and meat. Simmer until all the wine has evaporated and then add the stock and pour the contents on to the lamb bones.
4. Add the rosemary and thyme leaves, the bay leaves, and the chopped tomatoes, cover with a tightly fitting lid and bake in the oven for approximately 1½–2 hours.
5. Check to see if the lamb is tender but not breaking up. Remove the bones and bay leaves. Season to taste.
6. Cook the pasta according to pack instructions. Drain and add to the lamb ragout. Serve with grated pecorino sprinkled over.

Linguine with Mussels, Garlic & Fresh Tomato
Linguine alle Cozze Piccante

This great shaped pasta also goes well with pesto or clams, which you can substitute for the mussels. Make sure you get the shellfish from a good supplier and leave in salted water for a while as this will get rid of any grit inside the mussels.

Serves 4   Preparation time: 20 minutes + 30 minutes soaking

Cooking time: 15 minutes

350 g (12 oz) mussels

3 fat garlic cloves, unpeeled

60 ml (4 tablespoons) olive oil

1 fresh red chilli

4 bay leaves

125 ml (4 fl oz) good white wine

400 g (14 oz) baby plum tomatoes, halved lengthways

90 g (3 oz) sun-dried tomatoes, sliced

25 g (1 oz) fresh basil, stalks discarded

25 g (1 oz) fresh flat-leaf parsley, chopped finely

350 g (12 oz) linguine

salt and freshly ground black pepper

extra-virgin olive oil, to serve

1. Soak the mussels in salted water for 30 minutes to remove the grit, then wash in clean water and drain, removing any beards. Discard any mussels that have opened.
2. Bring a large pan of salted water to a rolling boil.
3. Place the unpeeled garlic cloves on a clean surface and crush with the blade of a heavy knife. Put the oil in a large non-stick frying pan and add the garlic, chilli and bay leaves. Cook for 1 minute over a low heat. Add the mussels, cover and cook for 2–3 minutes. Once opened (remove any mussels that have remained closed), pour in the wine and simmer for 3 minutes over a medium heat. Add the tomatoes, sun-dried tomatoes, basil and parsley and cook for a further 5 minutes over a low heat. Set aside.
4. Meanwhile, ease the pasta into the pan of boiling water and return to a rolling boil. Stir and cook for 5–8 minutes until al dente. Drain.
5. Remove the whole chilli from the sauce and then toss the pasta with the mussels. If you find there are too many shells, remove and discard some of them. Drizzle with extra-virgin olive oil and toss to mix. Adjust the seasoning and serve immediately.

Pasta

Pasta is at the heart of all Italian cooking. It is the first thing I remember helping my mother make when I was a child; there is nothing more satisfying than making your own pasta and cooking it immediately – the flavour and the texture seem so much better. You can hang fresh pasta until dry and then cook it or freeze it and, when you need to cook it, put the frozen pasta straight into boiling water. Pasta is what we call primi piatti (first course) which, strange as it may sound, is actually served after we have had antipasti, which is normally a mixture of hams and cheeses. The pasta is followed by the main course. I know it sounds like a lot of food but in Italy the portions are small and the sauce served with the pasta only coats it, so the meal is lighter than it sounds.

There are three main types of pasta:

Long pasta: spaghetti, vermicelli, fettuccine, lasagne, cannelloni, etc.
Short pasta: maccheroni, fusilli, penne, conchiglioni, etc.
Small pasta (suitable for soup): stelline, anelline, peperini, etc.

In Italy all dry pasta, by law, must be made from durum wheat and water, with the use of soft wheat flour allowed in the production of fresh pasta. Colour plays an important part in choosing pasta: a good pasta is a bright golden colour. Storing pasta is also very important: dry pasta should be kept in a dry clean place and away from fruit, rice and spices. Most dry pastas can be kept for an undetermined length of time but keep an eye on egg and spinach pasta, which will lose colour if exposed to light or kept long after the best-before date.

When cooking pasta it is best to use a large pan with plenty of water. The general rule is for every 100 g (3½ oz) of pasta use 1 litre (1¾ pints) of water and 10 g of salt; if you are serving the pasta with a strong sauce reduce the amount of salt. Once the water is boiling, add the pasta and stir with a fork, making sure it does not stick together; there is no need to add olive oil unless cooking lasagne sheets. In Italy we eat pasta when it is tender yet firm to the bite (al dente). Drain the pasta and add it to the sauce; this will give the pasta more flavour and slightly thicken the sauce. You can even finish cooking the pasta in the sauce.

Spring Tagliolini
Tagliolini Primavera

Primavera translates as spring and this dish gives you the chance to use all kinds of vegetables in season. I have chosen asparagus and peppers purely for flavour and also as they are my favourite vegetables, but use this as a guideline and go for it.

Serves 4   Preparation time: 25 minutes   Cooking time: 10 minutes

450 g (1 lb) asparagus
2 red peppers
2 yellow peppers
100 ml (3½ fl oz) extra-virgin olive oil
300 g (10 oz) tagliolini
1 medium courgette, sliced thinly
100g (3½ oz) mange tout, sliced thinly
100 ml (3½ fl oz) white wine
a cup of vegetable stock
200 g (7 oz) smoked mozzarella, diced
salt and freshly ground black pepper
4 flat-leaf parsley sprigs, to garnish

1. Preheat the oven to 200°C/fan oven 180°C/Gas Mark 6. Wash the asparagus and remove any tough base stalks; chop into bite-size pieces and place in a pan of boiling, salted water. Cook until tender – this will not take long – and plunge immediately into iced water.

2. Take the peppers and rub with some of the olive oil, place on a baking tray and cook whole in the oven for 20 minutes until the skin is blackened. Remove from the oven and place in a bowl, cover with cling film and leave for 10–15 minutes. Remove from the bowl and peel off the skin, which should come away easily. Chop and de-seed the peppers and set to one side.

3. Cook the pasta according to the pack instructions.

4. In a shallow pan, place 75 ml (3 fl oz) of the olive oil and heat until hot, then add the asparagus, peppers, courgette and mange tout and pasta and season to taste. Add the white wine and stock and simmer for 2 minutes; then add the smoked mozzarella, cook for 30 seconds and serve immediately, drizzled with the remaining olive oil and garnished with a sprig of flat-leaf parsley.

Conchiglioni with Gorgonzola & Walnuts
Conchiglioni al Gorgonzola e Noci

Serves 8   Preparation time: 10 minutes   Cooking time: 40 minutes

You can pretty much fill this pasta with anything from mince to parma ham or ricotta cheese and spinach. I decided to make a cheesy one. Some people find Gorgonzola too strong so dolcelatte may be better for you, but I love the taste of a strong, blue cheese; even Stilton would be great. Anyway, try it for yourself and see.

2 shallots, sliced very thinly

150 g (5 oz) sweet pancetta or smoked bacon, cubed

150 g (5 oz) walnuts, crushed

200 g (7 oz) Gorgonzola cheese

40 large pasta shells

10 sage leaves, chopped finely

5 ml (1 teaspoon) ground cinnamon

60 ml (4 tablespoons) grated parmesan cheese

For the béchamel sauce:

400 ml (14 fl oz) milk

40 g (1 ½ oz) butter

40 g (1 ½ oz) plain white flour

½ teaspoon grated nutmeg

salt and freshly ground black pepper

1. Preheat the oven to 200°C/fan oven 180°C/Gas Mark 6.
2. First make the béchamel. Heat the milk in a little saucepan and in another (one that is big enough to hold the milk), melt the butter over a low heat. Add the flour to the butter and mix with a whisk, then add the milk slowly, whisking all the time to avoid lumps. Carry on until the milk is finished.
3. Remove from heat and add the nutmeg and salt and pepper. Bring back to the boil but don't stop whisking. Cook for 2 minutes and leave to cool.
4. Sauté the shallots in a pan with the bacon and the crushed walnuts. Meanwhile, melt the Gorgonzola over a low heat, taking care not to burn the cheese (add a tablespoon of hot water if you need to).
5. Cook the pasta shells according to pack instructions, or until al dente. Drain and set aside.
6. Keep back some of the béchamel and mix the rest with the Gorgonzola and then add the bacon mix, sage and cinnamon. Fill the pasta shells with this mixture and place them in a ovenproof dish.
7. Pour the rest of the béchamel on top of the shells and sprinkle with parmesan. Season with salt and pepper and cook in the oven for 15 minutes. Serve immediately.

Rice & Gnocchi

Risotto is probably the most versatile of Italian dishes; you can pretty much use any meat, fish or vegetable. Make sure you get the right rice; Arborio and Vialone Nano are widely available. Making a perfect risotto should take 25 minutes from start to finish.

   Potato gnocchi are very easy to find if you don't want to make your own, but make sure you get a good brand. Gnocchi are cooked when they rise to the top of the pot, and you should drain and add them to the sauce immediately. But if you have the time always make your own – the results will be much better.

Risotto with Pumpkin & Crab
Risotto di Zucca e Granchio

The sweetness of the pumpkin really gives the crab some flavour. It is really important that you use fresh crabmeat in this recipe.

Serves 4   Preparation time: 10 minutes   Cooking time: 30 minutes

30 ml (2 tablespoons) extra-virgin olive oil

50 g (1³⁄4 oz) butter

4 banana shallots, chopped finely

450 g (1 lb) pumpkin, peeled, de-seeded and cut into 1 cm (¹⁄2-inch) cubes

2 garlic cloves, crushed

320 g packet of arborio risotto rice

250 ml (8 fl oz) white wine

1.5 litres (2³⁄4 pints) vegetable or fish stock

300 g (10¹⁄2 oz) crabmeat

45 ml (3 tablespoons) chopped fresh parsley

60 ml (4 tablespoons) grated parmesan cheese

salt and freshly ground black pepper

1. Heat the oil and half the butter in a large, deep frying pan, add the shallots and fry gently for 5 minutes, until soft. Stir in the pumpkin with the garlic and cook for 8 minutes, until it starts to soften. Add the rice and stir until the rice is glistening with butter; add the wine and cook until all the wine has been absorbed.

2. In a separate pan, bring the stock to a simmer.

3. Add a ladleful of hot stock to the rice and cook over a moderate heat for 3–5 minutes, stirring, until the liquid is absorbed. Add the crab, stir well and season with salt and ground black pepper.

4. Continue adding the stock, a ladleful at a time, until all or nearly all the stock has been used and the rice and pumpkin are tender (this should take 18 minutes from adding the first ladleful).

5. When the risotto is ready, remove from the heat and stir in the remaining butter, the parsley and the parmesan. The finished risotto should be quite fluffy but not soupy. Cover and leave for a minute and then serve.

Risotto with Spinach & Gorgonzola
Risotto al Bleu e Spinaci

This cheesy risotto should be quite creamy, so make sure when you are serving it that it is not too dry; you want a very fluffy consistency.

Serves 4   Preparation time: 10 minutes   Cooking time: 30 minutes

30 ml (2 tablespoons) extra-virgin olive oil
50 g (1³/₄ oz) butter
4 banana shallots, chopped finely
2 garlic cloves, crushed
320 g packet of arborio risotto rice
250 ml (8 fl oz) white wine
1 litre (1³/₄ pints) vegetable stock
450 g (1 lb) spinach
150 g (5½ oz) Gorgonzola cheese
45 ml (3 tablespoons) chopped fresh parsley
60 ml (4 tablespoons) grated parmesan cheese
salt and freshly ground black pepper

1. Heat the oil and half the butter in a large, deep frying pan, add the shallots and fry gently for 5 minutes until soft. Stir in the garlic and cook for 8 minutes until it starts to soften. Add the rice and stir until the rice is glistening with butter, add the wine and cook until all the wine has been absorbed.

2. In a separate pan, bring the stock to a simmer.

3. Add a ladleful of hot stock to the rice and cook over a moderate heat for 3–5 minutes, stirring, until the liquid is absorbed. Add the spinach and Gorgonzola, stir well and season with salt and ground black pepper.

6. Continue adding the stock, a ladleful at a time, until all or nearly all the stock has been used and the rice is cooked (this should take 18 minutes from adding the first ladleful).

7. When the risotto is ready, remove from the heat and stir in the remaining butter, the parsley and the parmesan. The finished risotto should be quite fluffy but not soupy. Cover and leave for a minute and then serve.

Seafood Risotto
Risotto Fruiti di Mare

Serves 4   Preparation time: 10 minutes   Cooking time: 50 minutes

1.5 litres (2¾ pints) fish stock
75 g (2¾ oz) butter
1 onion, finely diced
2 garlic cloves, finely diced
2 bay leaves, torn in half
300 g (10½ oz) arborio risotto rice
225 g (8 oz) mussels, scrubbed clean, beards and barnacles removed
150 ml (¼ pint) prosecco
175 g (6 oz) firm fish fillet, e.g. cod, salmon or haddock,
   skinned and cut in 5 cm (2-inch) pieces
30 ml (2 tablespoons) chopped fresh parsley
15 ml (1 tablespoon) snipped fresh chives
salt and freshly ground black pepper

1. Pour the stock into a large pan and bring to a gentle simmer.
2. Melt 25 g (1 oz) of the butter in a large pan, add the onion, garlic, and 2 bay leaf halves and sauté for 5–8 minutes, until soft. Stir in the rice. Cook, stirring, for about 30 seconds.
3. Gradually add the stock, a ladleful at a time, to the rice, stirring and adding more stock as each batch is absorbed. The total cooking time will be about 20 minutes, at the end of which the rice should be al dente. Season well to taste. Set aside.
4. Meanwhile, place the mussels in a separate pan, add the wine, cover tightly and cook over a high heat for 3–5 minutes, shaking the pan frequently, until the shells have opened. Strain the pan juices through a fine sieve and reserve. Discard any mussels that have remained closed.
5. Return the risotto to a low heat and stir in the remaining butter. Add some of the reserved pan juices if the risotto is a little dry. Stir in the fish, parsley and chives and season to taste. Cook for a further 1–2 minutes, until the fish is tender and just flakes. Discard the bay leaf halves.
6. Spoon the risotto into four large warmed bowls and arrange the mussels around the edge. Sprinkle with extra black pepper and serve immediately.

Parma Ham & Pesto Parcels
Portafoglio di Riso al Prosciutto e Pesto

If you are a vegetarian, thinly sliced courgettes or aubergine can be substituted for the parma ham. I love it like this as the ham gives so much flavour to the rice. Be careful with your seasoning as the parma ham is quite salty.

30 ml (2 tablespoons) extra-virgin olive oil

50 g (1 ³/₄ oz) butter

4 banana shallots, chopped finely

2 garlic cloves, crushed

320 g packet of arborio risotto rice

250 ml (8 fl oz) white wine

1.5 litres (2³/₄ pints) vegetable or fish stock

60 ml (4 tablespoons) chopped fresh basil

60 ml (4 tablespoons) grated parmesan cheese

salt and freshly ground black pepper

For the pesto:

25 g (1 oz) fresh basil leaves

30 ml (2 tablespoons) pine nuts

2 garlic cloves, chopped finely

250 ml (8 fl oz) extra-virgin olive oil

25 g (1 oz) parmesan cheese, grated

75 g (2³/₄ oz) pecorino cheese, grated

salt and freshly ground black pepper

To finish:

8 slices of parma ham

20 ml (4 teaspoons) grated parmesan cheese

1. Heat the oil and half the butter in a large, deep frying pan, add the shallots and fry gently for 5 minutes until soft. Stir in the garlic and cook for 8 minutes, until it starts to soften. Add the rice and stir until it is glistening with butter; add the wine and cook until all the wine has been absorbed.

2. In a separate pan, bring the stock to a simmer.

3. Add a ladleful of hot stock to the rice and cook over a moderate heat for 3–5 minutes, stirring, until the liquid is absorbed. Season with salt and pepper.

4. Continue adding the stock, a ladleful at a time, until all or nearly all the stock has been used and the rice is tender (this should take 18 minutes from adding the first ladleful).

5. When the risotto is ready, remove from the heat and stir in the remaining butter, the basil and the parmesan. The finished risotto should be quite fluffy but not soupy. Cover and set aside.

6. Meanwhile, put all the ingredients for the pesto into a food processor and blitz until combined.

7. Take two pieces of parma ham and make a cross, then place a large dollop of risotto in the middle of the ham and wrap to make a parcel. Make the other three parcels in the same way.

8. Place a teaspoon of pesto on top of the parcel with a spoonful of parmesan and grill for 2 minutes, until the cheese is bubbling.

Wild Mushroom Risotto
Funghi Selvatici e Olio di Tarfufo

Serves 4   Preparation time: 10 minutes   Cooking time: 35 minutes

30 ml (2 tablespoons) extra-virgin olive oil

25 g (1 oz) butter

4 banana shallots, chopped finely

450 g (1 lb) mixed wild mushrooms, sliced

2 garlic cloves, crushed

320 g packet of arborio risotto rice

250 ml (8 fl oz) white wine

1.5 litres (2¾ pints) vegetable or fish stock

15 ml (1 tablespoon) truffle oil

45 ml (3 tablespoons) chopped fresh parsley

60 ml (4 tablespoons) grated parmesan cheese

salt and freshly ground black pepper

1. Heat the oil and the butter in a large deep frying pan, add the shallots and fry gently for 5 minutes until soft. Stir in the mushrooms with the garlic and cook for 8 minutes, until they start to soften. Add the rice and stir until the rice is glistening with butter, add the wine and cook until all the wine has been absorbed.

2. In a separate pan, bring the stock to a simmer.

3. Add a ladleful of hot stock to the rice and cook over a moderate heat for 3–5 minutes, stirring, until the liquid is absorbed. Stir well and season with salt and ground black pepper.

4. Continue adding the stock, a ladleful at a time, until all or nearly all the stock has been used and the rice is ready (this should take 18 minutes from adding the first ladleful).

5. When the risotto is ready remove from the heat and stir in the truffle oil, parsley and parmesan. The finished risotto should be quite fluffy but not soupy. Cover and leave for 1 minute and then serve.

Gnocchi

Serves 4   Preparation time: 15 minutes   Cooking time: 40 minutes

1 kg (2 lb 4 oz) large, floury potatoes, e.g. king edwards
2 egg yolks
200 g (7 oz) plain flour, plus extra for rolling
1 litre (1¾ pints) water or chicken stock, for poaching
salt

1. Cook the unpeeled potatoes in a pan of boiling, salted water for about 30 minutes, until soft. Drain and place in the oven for 5 minutes to dry. Allow to cool enough for you to handle. Peel the potatoes and mash or press through a potato ricer into a bowl. Season with salt and then beat the egg yolks and flour into the potatoes, a little at a time. This will form a smooth, slightly sticky dough.

2. Tip out on to a well floured board, then roll the dough into long sausages about 1 cm (½ inch) thick and cut into sections about 2 cm (¾ inch) long. Place each piece on a fork and press down with your thumb; then roll on to the board, leaving grooves on one side of the gnocchi.

3. In a large pan, bring the water or stock to the boil. Add the gnocchi, about 40 at a time, cook until they rise to the surface and then cook for another 50–60 seconds. Remove with a slotted spoon to a large bowl and keep warm while cooking the remaining gnocchi. Repeat this procedure until all the gnocchi are done. Serve with any of the sauces in this chapter.

Wild Mushroom Sauce
Funghi Selvatici

I love mushrooms and this is a very versatile sauce; serve with the gnocchi opposite, or with pasta, fish or steak. Why not roast some salmon and serve this sauce on top, like I did the other day?

Serves 4   Preparation time: 10 minutes   Cooking time: 20 minutes

75 ml (5 tablespoons) extra-virgin olive oil

1 small onion, chopped finely

1 garlic clove, crushed

4 field mushrooms, sliced

175 g (6 oz) wild mushrooms, sliced

60 ml (4 tablespoons) chopped fresh flat-leaf parsley

125 ml (4 fl oz) dry white wine, e.g. Verdicchio

125 ml (4 fl oz) vegetable stock

8 fresh basil leaves, chopped

50 g (1¾ oz) pecorino cheese, grated

salt and freshly ground black pepper

1 quantity cooked gnocchi, opposite

fresh basil leaves, torn, to garnish

grated parmesan cheese, to serve

1. Heat 45 ml (3 tablespoons) of oil in a large frying pan on a low heat, add the onion and garlic and fry for 5 minutes, until soft and just starting to brown.

2. Stir in the mushrooms and parsley and fry for 5–8 minutes, until the mushrooms are golden brown. Season.

3. Add the wine and stock and simmer for 5 minutes. Remove from the heat and stir in the basil and pecorino cheese. Add more seasoning, if necessary. Add to the gnocchi and serve, sprinkled with some torn basil leaves and with some grated parmesan cheese on top. This goes well with a tomato and basil salad.

Shrimps & Rocket
Gamberetti e Rucola

Serves 4   Preparation time: 15 minutes   Cooking time: 20 minutes

For this recipe you can use any prawns: if you fancy splashing out on tiger prawns go ahead, but shrimps are a great inexpensive option.

15 ml (1 tablespoon) extra-virgin olive oil

30 ml (2 tablespoons) chopped onion

1 garlic clove, crushed and peeled

200 ml (7 fl oz) dry white wine

6 ripe Italian plum tomatoes, skinned, de-seeded and finely chopped

200 g (7 oz) shrimps

150 ml (¼ pint) double cream

1 quantity cooked gnocchi, page 88

a handful of rocket, chopped

15 ml (1 tablespoon) chopped fresh basil

1. Heat the oil in a frying pan and sauté the onion, add the garlic and cook for 3–4 minutes.
2. Remove the garlic and then add the wine and cook until it has almost all evaporated.
3. Add the tomatoes and cook for 10 minutes, stirring with a wooden spoon. Then add the shrimps and cream. Cook until the cream has reduced a little, add the cooked gnocchi, sprinkle with rocket and basil, stir and serve.

Four Cheese Sauce
Quattro Formaggi

This sauce is very rich so serve it with a nice salad as one dish. If you can't find any of these cheeses just increase the measurements of any of the others.

Serves 4   Preparation time: 5 minutes   Cooking time: 12 minutes

75 g (2 ³/₄ oz) **parmesan cheese, grated**
25 g (1 oz) **Gorgonzola cheese, crumbled**
50 g (1³/₄ oz) **Taleggio cheese, cubed**
50 g (1³/₄ oz) **mozzarella cheese, grated**
125 ml (4 fl oz) **milk**
25 g (1 oz) **plain white flour**
25 g (1 oz) **white breadcrumbs**
¹/₂ teaspoon **mustard powder**
salt and freshly ground black pepper
1 **egg**
1 **quantity cooked gnocchi, page 88**
chopped fresh flat-leaf parsley, to garnish

1. Melt all the cheeses with the milk over a low heat and bring to a soft boil; then add the flour, breadcrumbs, mustard powder and seasonings.
2. Cook for 2–3 minutes, stirring well. Leave to cool before adding the egg. Then beat in the egg and heat through gently.
3. Pour over the cooked gnocchi and serve with a sprinkling of chopped parsley.

Tomato, Mozzarella & Basil Sauce
Pomodoro, Mozzarella e Basilico

Simplicity at its best: great ingredients will always make great recipes. This one is a prime example.

Serves 4   Preparation time: 5 minutes   Cooking time: 35 minute

60 ml (4 tablespoons) olive oil

1 small onion, chopped finely

1 garlic clove, crushed

400 g can of chopped tomatoes

a bunch of fresh basil, leaves torn

2 bay leaves

1 quantity cooked gnocchi, page 88

8 slices of mozzarella cheese

salt and freshly ground
    black pepper

1. Heat the oil in a large, deep pan, add the onion and cook over a very low heat for 5 minutes, until soft but not brown.

2. Stir in the garlic, tomatoes and basil. Add the bay leaves and cook over a low heat for 30 minutes until the sauce is very thick. Season well with salt and freshly ground black pepper. Remove the bay leaves and preheat the grill.

3. Mix the cooked gnocchi into the sauce and divide between four plates. Place two slices of mozzarella on each serving and place under the hot grill until the cheese is golden brown and bubbling. Serve immediately.

Duck Ragout
All'Anatra

In my village there is a restaurant that just serves this dish and the way they do it is by cooking the whole bird in the tomato sauce. You have the pasta with the sauce to start and the meat with the salad as a main course.

Serves 4   Preparation time: 5 minutes   Cooking time: 1 hour

5ml (1 teaspoon) olive oil

500 g (1 lb 2 oz) boneless duck
    breasts, skinned and cubed

1 onion, chopped

1 garlic clove, crushed

60 ml (4 tablespoons) good
    red Italian wine

1 large jar of tomato passata

salt and freshly ground
    black pepper

1 quantity cooked gnocchi, page 88

chopped fresh flat-leaf parsley,
    to garnish

grated parmesan cheese, to serve

1. Heat the oil in a saucepan, add the duck, onion and garlic and cook for 10 minutes, stirring occasionally, until browned. Deglaze the pan with the red wine and then add the passata.

2. Bring to the boil and simmer for 50 minutes on low heat, until the meat is tender. Add seasoning to taste. Mix with the cooked gnocchi and serve immediately, topped with chopped parsley and grated parmesan.

Italian Rice

Rice, as we all know, originated in Asia but has been grown in Italy since AD 1550, mainly in the northern regions of Italy near the river Po. Italy is now the main rice-producing country in Europe, with Spain running a close second. What this means is that the average Italian will eat 5 kg of rice per year and in the north it is almost overtaking pasta as the national dish.

As with pasta there are many different varieties of rice but I am only going to mention the three that I would use. **Arborio** is the most commonly available; it has long, plump grains and is mainly used in the making of risottos. The cooking time is generally 14–15 minutes.

Pandano is a small, fairly long-grained rice and, although it is quite plump, it cooks in 13–14 minutes and is best used for soups and minestrone.

I consider **carnaroli** to be the king of rice varieties for risotto. It is less widespread than the above varieties and cultivation is limited. It cooks in 16–18 minutes.

Although I have given you cooking times, the best way to tell if your rice is cooked is to keep trying it. You want rice to be tender, yet firm, without a chalky centre – and personal taste is obviously very important. A good risotto will take 25 minutes, no less and no more.

Italian rice must never be washed before cooking, or the rice will retain water and not absorb the stronger flavours of the cooking liquid. During cooking the pan must remain uncovered. Rice, like pasta, continues cooking after you remove it from the heat, so it should either be served immediately or removed when it is al dente, to stop it from overcooking. Drizzle the rice with olive oil if you want to use it later on; this will keep it fresh.

Not many people are aware of the versatility of rice: it is great as a savoury dish but fantastic as a sweet dish. Because rice is extremely delicate and almost neutral in flavour it combines really well with sugar, honey, almonds and all fruits to make delicious desserts.

Italian Tomatoes

This fruit comes in all shapes and sizes but, in season, it is an unbeatable ingredient and probably the most versatile for Italian cooking – from pasta sauces to simple salads or, as I used to have it when I got back from school, just on toasted bread with a touch of extra-virgin olive oil (**bruschetta**). Our garden always had tomatoes, wild rocket and courgette flowers and great watermelons in the summer.

I would love to share with you some ideas of how my mother used to make the best use of tomatoes in season. Just chop 2 or 3 tomatoes in a bowl, and add some finely chopped garlic and onion or shallots with some ripped basil and lots of extra-virgin olive oil. Not only can you put it on bread but I also love it on boiled hot pasta, especially on penne in the summer with some grated parmesan; very quick, very tasty and healthy for the kids, stopping them from snacking on crisps or chocolate bars when they come back from school. Of course, you can cook the same mix for about 5 minutes, adding a little water from the pasta and maybe half a vegetable stock cube for taste, which turns it into a great meal.

My favourite has to be the **plum tomato**, which originated in Eurasia and has been grown in Europe for ever. It is primarily grown in the regions of Emilia Romagna and Campania, with a smaller shares of the market taken up by Piemonte and Lazio. I love roasting plum tomatoes. All you have to do is cut them in half and top with a sprinkle of breadcrumbs, olive oil and a little parmesan and roast them until they become soft; serve them with a poached egg for breakfast, again very healthy and quick.

As for cherry tomatoes, which seem to be all over the supermarkets, again they are a great snack just as they are or chopped in salads with some roasted peppers and buffalo mozzarella.

Tomatoes for cooking should be a deep red, which means they are ripe; but for salads go for the lighter reds because they are not as ripe and will not be as watery. Italian production of tomatoes is mostly for the home market, where we sell them fresh, canned or dried. Export to the UK in the 80s was only 20% of the production. We are lucky nowadays to have lots more, especially in season.

If you need to make a tomato-based sauce and you are short of time, the best thing to do is buy a passata sauce from your supermarket, add the rest of your ingredients and away you go. I love passata so much, I now bottle my own.

I could go on for hours about this wonderful fruit, which I could not live without, but it is time to move on.

Fish

This chapter has to be my **favourite** - not only because of the way I was brought up, eating lots of fish, but also because of my fish restaurants. Sadly in this country people don't really eat that much fish, but now with my help and the help of Rick Stein things are improving all the time. So please don't shy away from the fish counters in your supermarket. Listen to the trained staff and you will find yourself changing your diet to include more fish. It is so easy to cook as well as being **very good for you**.

Some of the recipes in this chapter use a whole fish. If you don't want to have to deal with the bones, ask your fishmonger for fillets; cook them in the same way as whole fish, but reduce the cooking time or the fish will be overcooked.

Adriatic Fish Stew
Zuppa di Pesce dell'Adriatico

*'Stew' is not my
favourite word; sadly,
this is not a great
translation of the name
of this wonderful dish.
My recommendation is
to have a look at the
fish listed here and
then see if you can find
it. Otherwise make up
your own version with
whatever fish you can
find or prefer.
Basically, treat this
recipe as a guideline.*

Serves 4   Preparation and cooking time: 1³/₄ hours

1 onion, chopped roughly

1 carrot, chopped roughly

2 celery sticks, chopped roughly

6 mushrooms

400 g (14 oz) whole small fish, e.g. mackerel, red mullet or sea bream, cleaned and scaled, heads removed

3 garlic cloves

400 g (14 oz) live mussels

500 ml (18 fl oz) dry white wine

90 ml (3½ fl oz) extra-virgin olive oil

3 garlic cloves, chopped

300 g (10½ oz) small squid, cleaned and cut in 1 cm (½-inch) pieces

300 g (10½ oz) raw prawns, shelled and de-veined

400 g (14oz) fresh, ripe tomatoes (preferably Italian plum), peeled and chopped

2 medium-hot red chillies, de-seeded and chopped

25 g (1 oz) saffron strands

500 g (1 lb 2 oz) assorted fish fillets, e.g. sea-bass, sole, cod, grey mullet or red mullet, cut in 3 cm (1½-inch) pieces

salt and freshly ground black pepper

25 g (1 oz) fresh flat-leaved parsley, chopped, to garnish

1. Place the onion, carrot, celery, mushrooms, small fish and whole garlic cloves in a pan and cover with 1 litre (1³/₄ pints) of cold, slightly salted water. Bring to the boil, reduce the heat immediately and simmer for 20 minutes.

2. Meanwhile, wash and scrape the mussels (discard any open mussels as they are no good). Heat a heavy-bottomed pan, place the cleaned mussels inside, cover and cook for 2–3 minutes, until they begin to open. Add a quarter of the white wine and cook until all the mussels are cooked and open (discard any that are not open). Strain the mussel stock and remove the mussels from their shells (leaving eight in the shell for the garnish). Add the mussel stock to the pan of whole fish, but keep the mussels to one side.

3. Place the extra-virgin olive oil in a large pan, add the chopped garlic, the cleaned squid, shelled prawns, tomatoes and chillies. Stir in the remaining white wine, cover the pan and simmer for 15 minutes. Add salt and pepper to taste and the saffron.

4. Remove the whole fish from the stock, separate the fish from the bones and discard the bones.

5. Place the fish fillets in the pan of squid and prawns in tomato sauce and then add the stock, mussels and pieces of whole fish. Correct the seasoning. Garnish with chopped parsley and the mussels in the shells.

Squid Stuffed With Ricotta & Parmesan
Calamari Ripieni

Squid is probably the most versatile fish on the market, but you have to be careful when cooking it: if you cook it too long the squid will become very hard, if you cook it too little it will be rubbery! This recipe is very popular in my restaurant, Zilli Fish, but I am pretty sure that everybody's favourite is still deep-fried with tartare sauce; for calamari fritti just dust the squid rings with seasoned flour and deep-fry for 3 minutes. Have a go, it's easy to do and fantastic to eat.

Serves 4   Preparation time: 10 minutes   Cooking time: 45 minutes

8 squid about 15 cm (6 inches) long, cleaned (keep tentacles)

500 g (1 lb 2 oz) ricotta cheese

800 g (1³/₄ lb) spinach, washed, dried and chopped finely

75 g (2³/₄ oz) parmesan cheese, grated

freshly ground black pepper

¹/₂ teaspoon grated nutmeg

40 g (1¹/₂ oz) fresh flat-leaved parsley, chopped

1 egg, beaten lightly

60 ml (4 tablespoons) olive oil

2 garlic cloves, minced finely

500 g (1 lb 2 oz) plum tomatoes, peeled and puréed in a blender

15 ml (1 tablespoon) tomato purée

¹/₂ teaspoon chopped fresh rosemary

1. Preheat the oven to 160°C/fan oven 140°C/Gas Mark 2. Cut off the squid tentacles so you just have the body cavity; make sure you keep it whole so you can stuff it without it leaking.

2. Mix together the ricotta, spinach, parmesan, pepper, nutmeg, parsley and egg. Set aside.

3. Heat 2 tablespoons of the oil in a shallow saucepan over medium heat, add the garlic and cook for 20 seconds and then add the blended tomatoes. Bring to the boil and add the tomato purée, lower the heat and add the rosemary. Simmer the sauce for 25 minutes, stirring occasionally.

4. While the sauce is simmering, stuff the body of each squid with the spinach and cheese mix until they are each one-third full (if overstuffed they will split). Poke one or two holes into the body of each squid. Fasten the opening of each squid with a toothpick or cocktail stick.

5. Take a shallow ovenproof frying pan, add the remaining olive oil and, on a high heat, cook the squid until brown all over. Finish in the oven for 4–6 minutes.

6. Just before serving add the tentacles to the sauce and cook for 1 minute. Pour the sauce around the stuffed squid and serve.

Fish & Fishing

It is not surprising to learn that fish has always paid an important role in the Italian diet, when thousands of kilometres of the country are coastline! Mediterranean fish is quite low in fat and rich in taste that is reminiscent of the sea and seaweed; for this reason it is particularly suitable for simple preparations without the use of heavy sauces. It is well known that fish is an essential raw material for a healthy diet; it has a high protein content and a remarkable content of phosphorus when compared to other foods. On top of all that, it is also low in calories and is very easy to digest.

When buying fish there are certain indications of how fresh the fish is. The first and easiest to recognise is the smell: the fishier it smells, the older the fish is. If you are buying a whole fish, make sure you buy a fish with bright eyes, shiny scales and rose-coloured gills, which indicate that the fish is fresh. If you are still not sure, poke the fish with your finger: it should be firm to the touch.

Every time I hear the word 'fishing' I shiver, remembering those dark cold mornings boarding this little fishing boat as we went off to sea. If we were lucky we would come back with a lunch of maybe some hake or sea-bass, but always mussels from near the shore on the rocks and lots of baby clams and razor clams for my mom's pasta sauce. Then I would go and help the local fishmonger prepare the fish and, at the end of the day, he would pay me with a bucket of fish. Thinking back now, I realise that my diet was really healthy, which I took for granted until I left home.

I was helping the fishermen during the school holidays between the ages of 12 and 14 and I wish that nowadays more young people got involved in eating and cooking fish. It's very important that you start your children eating fish at a young age, as I did with my daughter Laura; what I had to do was to hide the fresh fish in the pasta sauces so that she wouldn't notice – for example, fresh tuna with tomato sauce or salmon or bass, but the best and the cheapest fish that I would recommend have to be mackerel or sardines, oily fish that are extremely good for the brain and skin. Sadly, these days most fish, especially cod, are very expensive, due to overfishing. Let's hope that there will always be plenty of fish in the sea.

Hake in Cherry Tomato & Wine Broth
Nasello in Guazzetto

This fish dish was one of my first recipes when I was a junior in a hotel on the Adriatic coast – very popular because the fish is caught just off shore. It was on the menu quite a lot, served with many different sauces, but this was the best combination as far as I was concerned.

Serves 4   Preparation time: 20 minutes   Cooking time: 25 minutes

60 ml (4 tablespoons) extra-virgin olive oil
1 small red onion, diced finely
1 garlic clove, crushed
leaves of 1 fresh rosemary sprig, chopped
4 x 200 g (7 oz) hake fillets
1 carrot, diced finely
2 celery sticks, trimmed and diced finely
350 g (12 oz) cherry tomatoes, halved
100 ml (3½ oz) dry white wine
450 ml (16 fl oz) fish stock
45 ml (3 tablespoons) fresh thyme leaves
8 fresh sage leaves, chopped finely
sea salt and freshly ground black pepper

1. Preheat the oven to 200°C/fan oven 180°C/Gas Mark 6. Take an ovenproof pan and place over a low heat, heat 30 ml (2 tablespoons) of oil in it and sauté the onion, garlic and rosemary for 5–6 minutes until soft.
2. Cut the fillets in half. Season the fish with salt and freshly ground black pepper. Add the fish to the onion mixture and cook for 3–4 minutes, turning the fish several times.
3. Stir in the remaining vegetables, tomatoes and wine; simmer for 5 minutes to reduce the wine. Add the stock and herbs and bring to the boil.
4. Transfer the fish to the oven and cook for 15 minutes until the fish is cooked through. Spoon the fish and vegetables into the centre of four shallow bowls and then gently spoon over the broth. Drizzle over the remaining olive oil to serve.

Turbot Roasted with Potatoes
Rombo al Forno con Patate

Serves 4   Preparation time: 10 minutes   Cooking time: 35 minutes

This fish is a little on the expensive side but worth it as a special occasion or a Sunday lunch; yes, I did say Sunday lunch – there is no need to have roast beef, lamb or pork when you can have this wonderful fish as a centrepiece, with lots of vegetables.

500 g (1 lb 2 oz) desiree potatoes, peeled, sliced finely, rinsed and dried

60 ml (4 tablespoons) extra-virgin olive oil

6 garlic cloves, unpeeled, crushed with the back of a knife

leaves of 25 g (1 oz) fresh sage sprigs

leaves of 25 g (1 oz) fresh thyme sprigs

leaves of 25 g (1 oz) fresh rosemary sprigs

4 whole turbot, weighing about 400 g (14 oz) each, gutted and scaled

juice of 1 lemon

salt and freshly ground black pepper

To serve:

4 x 100 g (3½ oz) packets of fresh watercress

2 lemons, halved

1. Preheat the oven to 200°C/fan oven 180°C/Gas Mark 6. In a roasting tray, place the sliced potatoes, drizzle with olive oil, sprinkle with salt and pepper and add the garlic cloves and half the herbs. Do not layer the potatoes on top of each other but leave as a single layer. Place in the bottom of the oven and cook until golden and crisp, approximately 15–20 minutes. Discard the garlic cloves.

2. Meanwhile, slash the turbot with a sharp knife, stuff with the remaining sage, rosemary and thyme and season. Place the fish on top of the potatoes and splash with olive oil. Transfer the tray to the top of the oven and cook until crisp and golden, approximately 10–15 minutes.

3. While the fish is cooking, wash the watercress and trim the ends with a pair of scissors. Divide between four plates. Place the turbot on top and pile crisp potatoes next to the turbot. Drizzle with olive oil and serve with half a lemon per person.

Roasted Sea-Bass & Fennel
Spigola al Finocchio

When I was a child working for the local fisherman, bass was always one of the most popular fish on the market. You can cook bass in so many ways, or even eat it raw when it is very fresh, thinly sliced and dressed with a little soy, lemon and coriander. Fennel is another one of my favourite vegetables and sea-bass is definitely my favourite fish, so this for me is a marriage made in heaven.

Serves 6   Preparation time: 15 minutes   Cooking time: 40 minutes

2 baking potatoes, peeled and sliced 1 cm (½ inch) thick

1.4 kg (3 lb) whole sea-bass, scaled and gutted

2–4 small fresh rosemary sprigs, plus extra to garnish

2 garlic cloves, sliced thinly

½ lemon, sliced thinly

90 ml (3½ fl oz) olive oil

2 fennel bulbs

20 g (scant 1 oz) fennel seeds

sea salt and freshly ground black pepper

1. Preheat the oven to 240°C/fan oven 220°F/Gas Mark 9. Par-boil the sliced potatoes for 2 minutes and then drain.
2. Make diagonal incisions across each side of the fish, making sure not to go through to the bone. Wash and dry.
3. Place a small sprig of rosemary and a slice of garlic in each slit, and put the remaining garlic and rosemary and the lemon into the cavity of the fish.
4. Rub the fish with 60 ml (4 tablespoons) of olive oil and sprinkle with sea salt, half the fennel seeds and pepper.
5. Slice the fresh fennel lengthways into 1 cm (½-inch) thick pieces. Place the potatoes and fennel in a baking tray and sprinkle with the remaining fennel seeds, salt and pepper. Place the fish on top and drizzle again with the remaining olive oil.
6. Cover the tray with foil and bake for approximately 35 minutes.
7. Remove and serve on a plate with potatoes and fennel set around the fish and garnished with a sprig of rosemary.

Plaice Fillets Rolled with Cabbage, & Prosecco Sauce
Rotolo di Platessa e Verza Salsa di Prosecco

This wonderful flat fish is well known in my country, where you can find it in any fish shop. This recipe, if you have the time, is quite fantastic and any sparkling wine will do if you can't find prosecco, or even white wine. So, give it a go and really impress your friends – or stick to your fish and chips.

Serves 4   Preparation time: 15 minutes   Cooking time: 15 minutes

8 small plaice fillets

8 large cabbage leaves

For the stuffing:

25 g (1 oz) butter

1 small onion, chopped finely

1 garlic clove, chopped finely

3 sun-dried tomatoes, chopped

45 ml (3 tablespoons) lemon thyme leaves

50 g (1³/₄ oz) wholemeal breadcrumbs

juice of 1 lemon

salt and freshly ground black pepper

For the prosecco sauce:

1 bottle of prosecco

a pinch of saffron strands (optional)

15 ml (1 tablespoon) olive oil

1 garlic clove, crushed

3 banana shallots, roughly chopped

¹/₂ lemon grass stick, smashed

200 ml (7 fl oz) fish stock

250 ml (9 fl oz) double cream

juice of 1 lemon

1. First make the stuffing. Place the butter in a pan and let it melt over the heat until it begins to froth, add the onion and garlic and sauté, stirring, for 3–4 minutes until soft. Remove from the heat. Then add the tomatoes, thyme, breadcrumbs and lemon juice. Season to taste and set aside to cool for about 10 minutes.

2. Put the large cabbage leaves into boiling, salted water for 2 minutes until al dente, then plunge into iced water and pat dry. Put a cabbage leaf on a piece of cling film and lightly season with salt and pepper (make sure the cling film is slightly larger than the cabbage leaf).

3. Put a plaice fillet on top of the cabbage (making sure the cabbage leaf is larger than the fish). Put a small ball of the stuffing mix on to one end of the plaice and, holding the cling film, roll up tightly, make sure that the cling film is only on the outside.

4. Repeat this eight times; this will give you two rolls per portion.

5. Put the bottle of prosecco in a pan and reduce by three-quarters to intensify the flavour; add the saffron at this stage if you have it.

6. Steam the fish in the cling film parcels for approximately 12–15 minutes.

7. In a separate pan, place the olive oil and heat. Slowly pan-fry the garlic, shallots and lemon grass for 4–5 minutes until soft. Add the reduced prosecco and fish stock to this mix and reduce again by one-third. Add the double cream and reduce by one-third again. Squeeze in some lemon juice and season with salt and pepper to taste. Pass through a sieve.

8. Remove the cling film from the rolls and slice each roll in half so you can see the layers. Pour the sauce over the fish and serve.

Salmon with Pancetta
Involtini di Salmone

I didn't cook salmon or smoked salmon until I came to the UK. My love for this wonderful fish came when I worked in a hotel in London. The chef was Scottish, so many recipes involved salmon and smoked salmon. I remember one day he roasted a whole side of smoked salmon with some cracked pepper on top; what a result, I thought. I still serve it every now and then in my restaurants.

Serves 4   Preparation time: 10 minutes + 30 minutes chilling
Cooking time: 15 minutes

800 g (1³/₄ lb) fresh salmon fillets (200 g/7 oz per portion)
8 thin slices of pancetta
30 ml (2 tablespoons) olive oil
25 g (1 oz) butter
1 garlic clove, chopped finely
350 g (12 oz) spinach, stalks removed
sea salt and freshly ground black pepper
extra-virgin olive oil, to serve

1. Preheat the oven to 200°C/fan oven 180°C/Gas Mark 6. Prepare the salmon fillet, slice into four portions equally, making sure all the bones are removed. Wrap two slices of pancetta around each piece of salmon, wrap in cling film individually and refrigerate for half an hour.

2. In a shallow, non-stick ovenproof pan, heat the oil on a medium heat. Season the salmon with pepper. Cook, presentation-side down, in the pan for 2 minutes and then transfer to the oven and bake for 4 minutes.

3. While the fish is cooking, melt the butter in another shallow pan and add the garlic. Stir for a few minutes and then add the spinach and cook on a medium heat. Remove from heat after 1 minute and it will wilt naturally. Season. Drain the spinach on kitchen paper and place in the middle of a plate, then place the salmon on top, drizzle with olive oil and serve.

Scallops Gratin
Capesante Gratinate

Serves 4   Preparation time: 15 minutes   Cooking time: 8 minutes

If you are lucky enough to find this great shellfish, then make sure the fishmonger has done all the work for you, in cleaning and getting rid of the sand. Do not soak them in water, keep them nice and dry. Before cooking, you can remove the coral if you don't like it and just cook the round scallops.

8 scallops, prepared
350 ml (12 fl oz) milk
40 g (1½ oz) butter
40 g (1½ oz) flour
50 g (1¾ oz) parmesan cheese, grated
50 g (1¾ oz) pecorino cheese, grated
30 ml (2 tablespoons) breadcrumbs
15 ml (1 tablespoon) chopped fresh herbs
salt and freshly ground black pepper

1. If you have the scallop shells, grease them; if not, use shallow individual ovenproof dishes.
2. Cut the scallops in half and poach in a little of the milk for 5 minutes. Drain and reserve the milk. Keep the scallops warm.
3. Take the reserved milk, add the remainder and enough extra milk to get 350 ml (12 fl oz) again. Melt the butter in a pan and stir in the flour. Cook for 1–2 minutes to make a roux and then gradually add the milk, stirring all the time to make sure there are no lumps. Bring to the boil and cook until thickened.
4. Add three-quarters of the cheeses and season with salt and pepper. Divide the scallops among the shells or dishes and pour over the sauce.
5. Mix the remainder of the cheese with the breadcrumbs and herbs and sprinkle over the top of the scallops. Brown under a hot grill and serve immediately.

Cod with Pesto Crust
Merluzzo al Pesto

Serves 4   Preparation time: 20 minutes   Cooking time: 15 minutes

4 x 150 g (5 ½ oz) cod fillets

For the pesto crust:
about 40 fresh basil leaves
3 garlic cloves, crushed
25 g (1 oz) pine nuts
50 g (1¾ oz) parmesan cheese, grated
45 ml (3 tablespoons) extra-virgin olive oil
40 g (1½ oz) butter
50 g (1¾ oz) wholemeal breadcrumbs
grated zest and juice of 1 lemon
salt and freshly ground black pepper

1. Preheat the oven to 200°C/fan oven 180°C/Gas Mark 6.

2. Rinse the basil leaves and then dry thoroughly on kitchen paper.

3. Place the basil leaves, garlic, pine nuts and parmesan in a food processor and blitz for 30 seconds. You can use a pestle and mortar but this will take a while.

4. Keep the food processor on and slowly add the olive oil until all is combined. Season to taste.

5. To make the crust, start by melting the butter in a large frying pan. When melted, remove from the heat and add the breadcrumbs, lemon juice and zest. Allow to cool and then mix with the pesto.

6. Pat firmly on the top of the cod fillets and bake in the oven for 15 minutes. Remove from the oven and serve with salad.

Well, this fish is definitely the bestseller in my fish restaurant, not done this way but deep-fried with chips. As an alternative, I give you this Italian recipe for cooking cod; my mom used to make the same dish but she used salt cod, which she soaked overnight and then made into this recipe.

Red Mullet with Olives & Capers
Triglie Puttanesca

Red mullet is the kind of fish that a lot of people get put off because of the bones but, if you are careful, you can enjoy a great recipe here, or you can get your fishmonger to fillet it for you.

Serves 4   Preparation time: 5 minutes + 30 minutes marinating
Cooking time: 10 minutes

2 x 450 g (1 lb) whole red mullet
125 ml (4 fl oz) + 15 ml (1 tablespoon) olive oil
60 ml (4 tablespoons) good white wine
120 ml (8 tablespoons) chopped fresh thyme
24 black olives, stoned and quartered
12 capers, chopped
sea salt and ground black pepper

1. Scale, gut and wash the mullet if the fishmonger has not already done so, and dry well. If you don't like dealing with the whole fish, get four fillets and the result will be the same.

2. Make three slashes diagonally on both sides of the mullet (do not go through to the bone). Place in a dish.

3. In a bowl, mix together the 125 ml (4 fl oz) of oil, wine and thyme, pour over the fish and leave to marinate for half an hour.

4. Heat the tablespoon of oil in a frying pan. Sprinkle the fish with sea salt and pepper and pan-fry for 7– 8 minutes on each side, basting all the time with the marinade.

5. Remove from the heat and keep the fish hot. Add the olives and the capers to the pan and cook for 2 minutes. Place the fish on a large platter and pour over the olive and caper sauce.

Poultry & Game

From the age of eleven I lived by the sea. I remember that before then we had lots of **wild boar**, **suckling pig** and, of course, organic chickens. My mother's favourite dish was made with **chicken** or **turkey**. She would quarter the whole bird and then cook it in a large pot covered with tomato sauce and herbs. When the meat was cooked, she would serve the sauce with some pasta and the meat as a main course with a nice fennel salad. Not only was it delicious, it was cheap and she could feed the whole family with the minimum of effort.

Chicken in Sea Salt & Pepper Crust
Pollo in Crosta di Sale e Pepe

Normally I would cook fish such as a sea bass or mullet this way, but at my house we kept chickens so every Sunday there was a different recipe with chicken. One day we created this one, it worked and I still like making it. Baking in salt keeps the chicken flesh very moist and tender; the skin does not go brown or crisp.

Serves 4   Preparation time: 15 minutes   Cooking time: 40–45 minutes

2 kg (4 ½ lb) chicken, cut in quarters

For the crust:
900 g (2 lb) coarse sea salt
75 g (2¾ oz) black peppercorns, crushed lightly
2 eggs, beaten

For the dressing:
175 ml (6 fl oz) extra-virgin olive oil
finely grated zest and juice of 1 lemon
90 ml (6 tablespoons) roughly chopped fresh flat-leaf parsley
freshly ground black pepper
green salad leaves, e.g. rocket or baby spinach,
**   and lemon wedges, to serve**

1. Preheat the oven to 200°C/fan oven 180°C/Gas Mark 6. Pat the chicken dry with kitchen paper. Mix together the sea salt, peppercorns and beaten eggs.
2. Line a large baking or roasting tray with foil. Spread a little of the salt mixture on the foil and place the chicken pieces on top. Press the remaining salt mixture all over the chicken pieces to completely enclose them. Bake for 30–40 minutes. The salt crust should feel hard and sound hollow when tapped.
3. Meanwhile, mix the oil, lemon zest and juice, parsley and black pepper in a small bowl.
4. As soon as you remove the chicken from the oven, scrape the salt crust off; it should come off the chicken in sections. Gently remove the chicken, making sure you leave the salt crust behind on the base of the dish.
5. Put all the chicken on a large platter and spoon over some of the dressing. Serve with a light green leaf salad, dressing and lemon wedges.

Marinated Leg of Wild Boar
Cinghiale Marinato

This is a very traditional regional dish in Abruzzo, where we have a national park in which you will find lots of these animals: restaurants in the area cook boar in all different sorts of ways as well as making a ham similar to parma ham that is lovely.

Serves 4–8   Preparation time: 10 minutes + overnight marinating
Cooking time: depending on weight, 1¹/₂–2¹/₂ hours

1.25 kg (2³/₄ lb) wild boar leg joint
440 ml (16 fl oz) Montepulciano D'Abruzzo red wine
15 ml (1 tablespoon) clear honey
15 ml (1 tablespoon) soft brown sugar
15 ml (1 tablespoon) wholegrain mustard
2 garlic cloves, chopped
leaves of 2 fresh rosemary sprigs, chopped
50 g (1³/₄ oz) butter
2 apples, peeled and quartered
125 g (4¹/₂ oz) soft brown sugar
15 ml (1 tablespoon) lemon juice

1. Place the boar in a crockery or glass dish. Combine the wine, honey, soft brown sugar, mustard, garlic and rosemary. Pour this over the joint and leave to marinate overnight, pouring the juices over periodically.

2. Preheat the oven to 190°C/fan oven 170°C/Gas Mark 5. Remove the boar from the dish, reserving the marinade. In a roasting tin, cook the boar for 30 minutes per 500 g (1 lb 2 oz) plus 30 minutes extra.

3. While the boar is cooking, strain the marinade into a saucepan and simmer until reduced by half. Then whisk in the butter but do not allow the sauce to boil.

4. In a dry frying pan, cook the apples for 2–3 minutes. Remove the apple pieces with a slotted spoon and drain off and discard half the liquid. Add the sugar and lemon juice to the remaining liquid and cook for 4 minutes; then return the apple to the pan. Cook the apple pieces until the juices begin to brown and caramelise and the apple pieces are coated in the caramelised juices.

5. Slice the boar and arrange on plates. Spoon over the sauce and add some pieces of caramelised apple.

Venison Loin with Marsala Sauce
Cervo al Marsala

Venison is like wild boar, in that is a great-tasting meat that we have in my region. Make sure you serve venison medium to medium-rare – in other words, not bloody – and make sure you get a good bottle of marsala as it will make a big difference to the flavour.

Serves 6   Preparation time: 30 minutes   Cooking time: 40–45 minutes

60 ml (4 tablespoons) extra-virgin olive oil
1 kg (2¼ lb) loin of venison
150 ml (¼ pint) port
150 ml (¼ pint) marsala
30 ml (3 tablespoons) redcurrant jelly
6 juniper berries, crushed
1 large garlic clove, chopped
salt and freshly ground black pepper

1. Preheat the oven to 220°C/fan oven 200°C/Gas Mark 7.
2. Heat 45 ml (3 tablespoons) of olive oil in a large, heavy-based flameproof roasting tin on the hob. Add the loin of venison and fry all over until sealed and golden brown. Remove the meat and set aside. De-glaze the roasting tin with the port and marsala, stirring constantly for 1 minute. Stir in the redcurrant jelly and continue to cook for 2 minutes until the juices are quite syrupy. Transfer to a small pan and set aside until required.

3. Put the remaining olive oil on a large piece of baking foil. Sprinkle the juniper berries and garlic over the foil and then season with salt and plenty of freshly ground black pepper. Place the venison in the centre and carefully wrap in the foil.

4. Place the venison parcel in a clean roasting tin and roast for 20 minutes.

5. Remove the meat from the oven and leave to rest for 15 minutes or so before carving (the venison should still be rare in the centre). Reheat the sauce to serve with the thinly sliced venison.

Turkey Parcels
Portafolglio di Tacchino

This is good way to serve turkey and prove that it's a good choice at any time of year. Serve with steamed spinach.

Serves 4   Preparation time: 5 minutes
Cooking time: 35 minutes + cooling

500 g (1 lb 2 oz) boneless turkey, cubed
100 g (3½ oz) unsalted butter, clarified (see note)
leaves of 1 fresh oregano sprig or 1 teaspoon dried oregano
300 g (10 oz) sun-dried tomatoes, chopped
50 g (1¾ oz) smoked mozzarella cheese, cubed
8 filo pastry sheets (keep moist by covering with a damp tea towel)
salt and freshly ground black pepper

1. Season the turkey with salt and pepper. Using about half the butter melted in a shallow frying pan, cook the turkey until golden brown. Remove from the heat and allow to cool. Mix the oregano and sun-dried tomatoes with the turkey. Using your hands, mix the smoked mozzarella with the turkey.

2. Take a sheet of filo pastry and place another on top, then put a quarter of the turkey/mozzarella mix in the middle. Brush around the corners with more of the clarified butter. Fold the edges up to make a square parcel and repeat with the remaining ingredients to make four parcels in total. Refrigerate for 1 hour.

3. Preheat the oven to 160°C/fan oven 140°C/Gas Mark 3.

4. Place the parcels on a baking tray, brush with the remaining butter and bake for 20–25 minutes or until golden brown on the outside and hot in the middle.

Note: To clarify butter, melt unsalted butter in a small saucepan and then pour off the golden, clear liquid on top, discarding the milky layer at the bottom.

Turkey Escalopes with Lemon Sauce
Scaloppa di Tacchino al Limone

Serves 4   Preparation time: 15 minutes   Cooking time: 10 minutes

Why do we wait until Christmas to eat this great meat and then overdose on it? I actually prefer to eat it at any other time. You can use it in the same way as chicken or veal, using the same cooking methods. Turkey escalope topped with mozzerella and parma ham is excellent as well and you don't have to eat turkey sandwiches for three days in a row.

4 x 225 g (8 oz) turkey escalopes
leaves of 1 fresh rosemary sprig, chopped finely
100 g (3½ oz) plain flour
2 eggs
100 g (3½ oz) dried breadcrumbs
45 ml (3 tablespoons) sunflower oil
50 g (1¾ oz) parmesan cheese, grated
salt and freshly ground black pepper
1 lemon, sliced, to garnish

For the lemon sauce:
30 ml (3 tablespoons) butter
15 ml (1 tablespoon) lemon juice
1 small onion, diced finely

1. Season each turkey escalope with salt and pepper. Sprinkle with the chopped rosemary.

2. Place the flour on a large flat plate, beat the eggs in a shallow bowl and spread the breadcrumbs on a third flat plate. First, coat each escalope in flour, then in the egg and finally in the breadcrumbs, pressing the breadcrumbs on to the escalope.

3. Preheat the grill to medium-hot. Heat half the oil in a large frying pan and add two escalopes. Fry for 2 minutes on each side until golden brown. Transfer to a foil-lined grill pan. Repeat with the remaining oil and escalopes.

4. Make the lemon sauce by melting the butter in a frying pan over medium heat. Add the lemon juice and onion and gently sauté until softened.

5. Sprinkle the escalopes with the parmesan cheese and grill for 1–2 minutes until the cheese is melted and bubbling. Serve the escalopes immediately, with the lemon sauce drizzled over and garnished with lemon slices.

Chicken Skewers with Rosemary
Spiedini di Pollo al Rosmarino

Serves 4   Preparation time: 20 minutes   Cooking time: 15–20 minutes

This recipe screams summer all the way. Make sure you marinate the chicken for at least one hour to enhance the flavour. Marinating in balsamic vinegar will give it a different flavour.

500 g (1 lb 2 oz) chicken breasts

Pesto Sauce (see page 84)

1 red pepper

1 yellow pepper

4 long rosemary twigs or
    wooden skewers

2 small courgettes, sliced

salt and freshly ground
    black pepper

For the marinade:

60 ml (1 tablespoons) olive oil

juice of 1 lemon

1. Mix the marinade ingredients together with salt and pepper, place the chicken breasts in it and leave to marinate for at least an hour.

2. Remove the chicken breasts from the marinade, reserving the marinade, and drain them well. Place between two sheets of cling film and beat with a

rolling pin until flattened and doubled in size. Spread the pesto over the breasts and roll up (like a swiss roll). Cut in pieces 4 cm (1 ¾ inches) thick.

3. Slice the peppers in half, de-seed and cut in large chunks. Remove the lower leaves from the rosemary 'skewers'. Pierce the pieces of chicken, courgettes, and peppers with a metal skewer, and then thread them on to the rosemary skewers.

4. Season lightly and brush the chicken and vegetables with the reserved marinade. Cook on a prepared barbecue or under a hot grill for 15–20 minutes, turning frequently and brushing with any remaining marinade, until the chicken is cooked and the vegetables are blackened.

Tuscan Chicken
Pollo alla Toscana

Everybody in Britain knows about Tuscany so I chose to do this recipe from this beautiful region. Porcini would be better fresh but dried ones will do. Serve with some roasted fennel. Great!

Serves 4   Preparation time: 30 minutes   Cooking time: 45 minutes

20 g (¾ oz) **dried porcini**

4 **tomatoes or** 300 g **canned, chopped tomatoes**

75 g (2¾ oz) **butter**

45 ml (3 tablespoons) **extra-virgin olive oil**

1.25 kg (2¾ lb) **chicken, jointed into 8 pieces**

a glass of dry white wine

1 **ladleful of chicken stock**

15 ml (1 tablespoon) **plain flour**

salt and freshly ground black pepper

1. Put the dried porcini in a saucepan and soften in tepid water to rehydrate them.

2. If you are using fresh tomatoes, pour boiling water over them, leave for a minute of so and then slash the skins and peel them. Remove the seeds and roughly chop the flesh.

3. Melt 25 g (1 oz) of the butter in a large saucepan with the olive oil, season the chicken pieces, add them to the pan and brown over a high heat, stirring frequently.

4. Pour in the wine and, when it has reduced by half, add the drained porcini, the tomatoes and the stock. Bring to the boil, reduce the heat and simmer for 45 minutes, or until the chicken is cooked.

5. Mix the remaining butter with a tablespoon of flour, add this to the pan and stir until the sauce is thick and velvety.

6. Transfer the chicken pieces to a serving dish and spoon the sauce over them. Serve with mashed potatoes or greens.

Quails Cacciatora
Quaglie alla Cacciatora

There's not too much meat on these little birds but what is there is delicious. I love serving them with polenta or wild mushrooms, a great marriage.

Serves 4   Preparation time: 15 minutes + 12 hours marinating
Cooking time: 15 minutes

4 quails on the bone
2 spanish onions
3 garlic cloves, chopped
½ head of celery
2 carrots
100 g (3½ oz) button mushrooms, sliced
100 g (3½ oz) black olives, stoned
1 fresh thyme sprig
2 fresh rosemary sprigs
12 cherry tomatoes
150 ml (¼ pint) olive oil
salt and freshly ground black pepper

For the marinade:
4 fresh thyme sprigs
4 garlic cloves
1 bottle of Barolo wine
250 ml (9 fl oz) red wine vinegar

1. Stuff the quails with the thyme and garlic from the marinade ingredients and place them in a container with the wine and red wine vinegar. Marinate for at least 12 hours.
2. Preheat the oven to 200°C/fan oven 180°C/Gas Mark 6.
3. Roughly chop the onions, garlic, celery and carrots in about 1 cm (½-inch) cubes. Place the vegetables on a roasting tray and add the sliced mushrooms, olives, thyme, rosemary and cherry tomatoes. Drizzle with a little olive oil and season well.
4. Place the quails on top of the vegetables and pour over the marinade; drizzle with the remaining olive oil and season with salt and pepper. Cook in the oven until golden brown, about 12–15 minutes.
5. Once cooked, remove the quails and keep warm. Strain the vegetables, retaining the cooking liquor, and keep the vegetables warm while you reduce the liquor by half.
6. Serve the quails with the vegetables on the side and the reduced sauce poured over.

Mom's Roasted Rabbit
Coniglio al Forno Mammamia

In my family we had rabbit two or three times a month because it was quite a cheap meat, so I developed a taste for it. Cooked properly, rabbit is very good and tender; as with any recipe, make sure you are using a good-quality wine.

Serves 4   Preparation time: 10 minutes   Cooking time: 1 hour

30 ml (3 tablespoons) black peppercorns

leaves of 2 fresh rosemary sprigs, chopped

2 garlic cloves, chopped

15 ml (1 tablespoon) sea salt

1.5 kg (3 lb 5 oz) rabbit, quartered

4 potatoes, peeled and quartered

60 ml (4 tablespoons) extra-virgin olive oil

8 plum tomatoes, halved, de-seeded and chopped roughly

100 ml (3½ oz) dry white wine

50 ml (2 fl oz) vegetable stock

1. Preheat the oven to 220°C/200°C fan oven/Gas Mark 7.
2. Crush the peppercorns with a pestle and mortar and then add the rosemary leaves, garlic and sea salt and crush again. Rub all over the rabbit pieces.
3. Take a large flameproof roasting tin and place on the hob. Heat the olive oil in it and then add the rabbit. Cook for about 5–7 minutes, until golden brown and crisp. Turn over and cook for a further 3 minutes.
4. Sprinkle the tomatoes over the rabbit, place the potatoes around and pour over the wine and vegetable stock. Bring to the boil and transfer the roasting tin to the oven. Bake for 50 minutes (if it becomes too dry add some more stock) until the rabbit is crisp and the potatoes are cooked through.
5. Serve in a shallow serving bowl with the juices poured over. Buttered tagliatelle goes well with this dish.

Game

Up until I was 11 years old we lived on a farm, so game was on the menu quite a bit; when in season we would have wild boar (cinghiale), rabbit (coniglio), hare (lepre) and so on. Just by the national park in my home region of Abruzzo, the boars run wild, with some culling being done. When you visit the region there are many restaurants that specialise in boar; they tend to serve it with fat pasta ribbons which can support the heavy sauce. In the past, hunting boar was a natural (and cheap) way of getting meat on the table and even now the average Italian eats it two or three times a year, the only difference being the growing concern for wildlife preservation, so hunting is carefully controlled. This is a dangerous sport as, when under pressure, the animal will attack. There is such a demand for wild boar that there are many boar farms, where the animals are kept in an enclosed wooded area leading a semi-wild life; the only problem with this, as with most farmed animals or fish, is that the flavour; is not as good. Wild boar sausages are also very popular, and they come either in a salami form or raw ready for grilling. They are delicious with polenta and thick gravy.

Wild rabbit or hare was another family favourite; we used to roast them in the oven with lots of white wine, olives, garlic, rosemary and potatoes. With hare, the best way was to make a hare ragù which we would have for Sunday lunch; it is a very filling dish when you serve it with pappardelle, which marries really well with game sauces.

Italian people love shooting; clay-pigeon shooting is only second in popularity to football in Italy, so by the time the real shooting season starts they are sharp shooters. I love eating pheasant, partridge and mallard; the taste is fantastic, but I personally couldn't shoot a fly! There is even a Festival of Thrushes in Montalcino, which takes place every year and is similar to a grouse hunt over here, although now they use farm-raised quails instead of wild birds.

Braised Chicken with Artichokes
Pollo Brasato ai Carciofi

This chicken recipe is great because the artichokes just give it that much more flavour and I would also add some new potatoes to this and turn it into a whole feast.

Serves 6   Preparation time: 30 minutes   Cooking time: 1 hour

3 globe artichokes

1 lemon, halved, zest removed and reserved

a bunch of fresh flat-leaf parsley, chopped finely

1 garlic clove, crushed

1 red onion, sliced thinly

500 ml (18 fl oz) chicken stock

6 boneless chicken breasts, with skin

salt and freshly ground black pepper

1. Start by preparing the artichokes: firstly, you need to trim the stalks and peel away a few of the tough outer leaves. Using a sharp knife, cut the tops off to expose the hearts. Rub the artichokes with a lemon half. Place the artichokes with the lemon half in a large pan of boiling water and cook for 15 minutes.

2. Drain the artichokes. Remove the hairy choke by holding the artichoke by the stalk with a clean cloth and scooping out the choke with a spoon.

3. Preheat the oven to 190°C/fan oven 170°C/Gas Mark 5. Make a gremolata by mixing the parsley, lemon zest and garlic. Cover and set aside until needed.

4. Place the onion in a roasting tin, pour in the stock and add the chicken, skin-side up. Take your other lemon half and cut it in half again. Add one quarter to the tin and squeeze the remaining quarter over the chicken.

4. Cut the prepared artichokes into quarters and add to the roasting tin.

5. Season and cover with foil. Cook in the oven for 20 minutes, and then remove the foil and cook for a further 30 minutes, until the chicken is thoroughly cooked and golden brown. Scatter with the gremolata to serve and accompany with Rosemary Roast Potatoes (page 178).

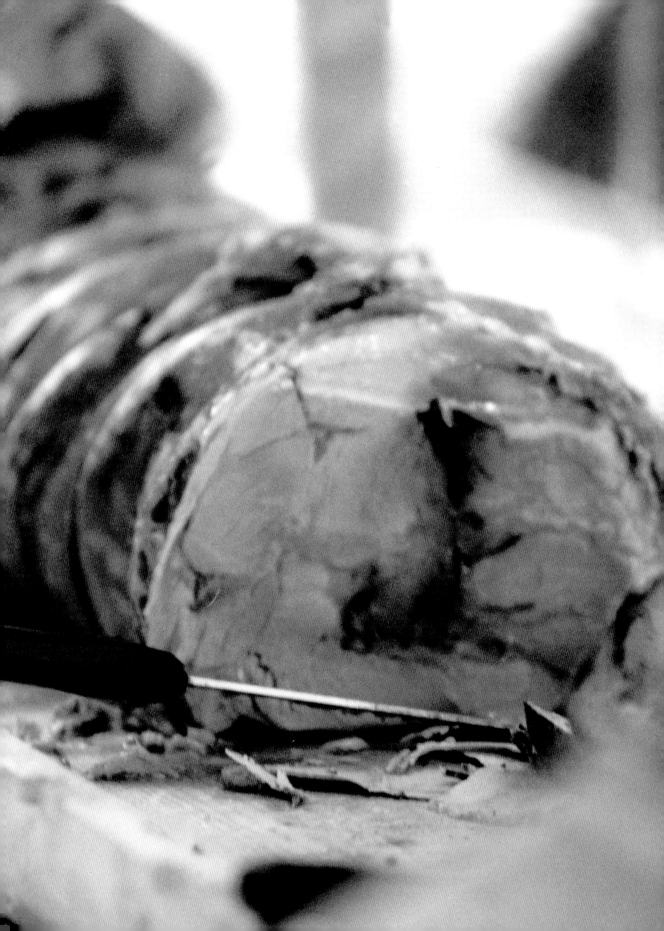

Meat

My favourite meat has to be **a nice juicy steak** and if it is a good, lean fillet steak, then I like it raw and sliced thinly on the plate with some chopped mushrooms, a little truffle oil and lemon. Always make sure you go to a **good butcher** and ask if the meat has been hung and treated in the right way. A good butcher can advise you on recipes for things like calves' liver, which is full of iron and tastes great with a few onions and some red wine, served with some mashed potatoes.

Veal Casserole
Vitello in Casseruola

Veal is not used a lot in England but I think this is a great shame as is such a tasty meat. Cooked this way, you can keep it for a couple of days before you reheat it and serve with some rice or pasta.

Serves 4   Preparation time: 10 minutes
Cooking time: 1 hour 20 minutes

30 ml (2 tablespoons) olive oil
2 onions, chopped
2 carrots, chopped roughly
1 celery stick, chopped
1 kg (2 lb 4 oz) veal loin, cubed
4 potatoes, cut into large dice

2 glasses of white wine
1 bay leaf
100 g (3½ oz) peas
salt and freshly ground
    black pepper

1. Preheat the oven to 180°C/fan oven 160°C/Gas Mark 4. In a flameproof casserole, heat the olive oil and then sauté the onions, carrots and celery until soft. Then add the veal pieces and cook until the veal is brown on all sides.
2. Remove from the heat and add the potatoes, wine, bay leaf and seasoning. Cover and cook in the oven for approximately 20 minutes.
3. Remove from the oven and stir, add the peas and return the veal to the oven.
4. Cook for a further hour, until the veal is lovely and tender.

Fillet of Pork Wrapped in Speck
Involtini di Maiale allo Speck

Speck is a German smoked ham which I discovered in my teenage years, whilst cooking at the Hilton in Munich, and then used for pasta sauces. If you can't find speck then use pancetta or smoked bacon. This is a great recipe because the cheese will give you all the flavour you need; again, if you can't find asiago then a good dolcelatte will do the job.

Serves 6   Preparation time: 20 minutes   Cooking time: 30 minutes

12 slices of pork fillet
12 slices of speck
12 slices asiago or similar cheese,
e.g. dolcelatte
12 fresh sage leaves
30 ml (2 tablespoons) plain
    white flour

45 ml (3 tablespoons) extra-virgin
olive oil
25 g (1 oz) butter
1 glass Moscato
1 ladleful of pork stock
salt and freshly ground
    black pepper

1. Flatten the fillet slices with a meat mallet and then cover each fillet with a slice of speck, a slice of cheese and a sage leaf. Roll up and secure with a toothpick to create a parcel.
2. Season the flour and place on a plate; roll each pork parcel in the flour, making sure the pork is lightly floured all over.

3. In a frying pan, heat the oil and butter and, when the butter starts foaming, add the pork parcels and brown at a high heat, turning them with a fork to make sure all sides are brown. Season.

4. Add the wine and leave to be absorbed by the pork, then add the stock and simmer, occasionally turning the involtini, for 15 minutes. When the sauce is reduced, remove the meat and place on a serving dish, pour over the sauce and serve.

Rack of Lamb with Rosemary
Carre d'Agnello al Rosmarino

I love this cut of lamb. You can make this an impressive centrepiece if you are cooking for a dinner party: serve the lamb on top of some vegetables with the potatoes all around and some fresh herbs to garnish the lamb — a very easy way to impress your friends.

Serves 8   Preparation time: 15 minutes   Cooking time: 20–25 minutes

1.4 kg (3 lb 2 oz) baking potatoes, peeled and quartered

100 g (3½ oz) dried breadcrumbs

leaves of 2 fresh rosemary sprigs, chopped

30 ml (2 tablespoons) chopped fresh flat-leaf parsley

30 ml (2 tablespoons) chopped fresh sage

1 fresh red chilli, de-seeded and chopped finely

60 ml (4 tablespoons) olive oil

900 g (2 lb) baby carrots with fronds, trimmed

8 baby aubergines

4 garlic cloves, lightly bashed

8 small racks of lamb (32 chops in total)

30 ml (2 tablespoons) smooth mustard

salt and freshly ground black pepper

For the gravy:

15 ml (1 tablespoon) balsamic vinegar

150 ml (¼ pint) red wine

150 ml (¼ pint) vegetable stock

25 g (1 oz) butter

1. Preheat the oven to 190°C/fan oven 170°C/Gas Mark 5. Bring a large pan of water to the boil and add the potatoes: par-boil for 10 minutes and then drain.

2. In a large bowl, mix the breadcrumbs, herbs and chilli, season with salt and freshly ground black pepper and set aside.

3. Place half the oil in a large roasting tin and heat in the oven for 5 minutes until very hot and almost smoking. Quickly add the potatoes, baste in the hot oil and cook for 15 minutes. Then add the carrots, aubergines and garlic. Roast for about 15 minutes, until cooked.

4. Meanwhile, heat the remaining oil in a large ovenproof pan and seal the racks of lamb all over for 5–8 minutes. Transfer the lamb to the oven and roast for 8 minutes for medium rare to 12 minutes for well done.

5. Remove the lamb from the oven and spread the mustard on it and then press the breadcrumb mixture on to the meat. Return to the oven and roast for a further 5 minutes. Remove and allow to rest.

6. While the meat is resting, make the gravy. Pour off and discard as much fat as possible from the pan and place on the hob. Add the vinegar to the pan and de-glaze, scraping the roasting meat 'bits' off the base. Stir in the red wine and stock and boil for 5 minutes, until syrupy. Take off the heat and whisk in the butter. Strain through a sieve and serve with the meat and vegetables.

Baby Goat or Mutton Stew
Capretto al Vino

When I put baby goat on my menu in the 8os, my friends told me no English people would touch it. How wrong were they! It sold, not too quickly I admit, but slowly I gained people's confidence and it sold more and more – so much so that I decided to share it with you.

Serves 4   Preparation time: 30 minutes   Cooking time: 2 ³/₄ hours

2 kg (4 lb 8 oz) boneless baby goat (kid or chevron) or mutton

30 ml (2 tablespoons) olive oil

4 onions, diced roughly

4 carrots, chopped roughly

4 celery sticks, sliced fairly thickly

1 swede, chopped roughly (optional)

a glass of red wine

150 ml (¹/₄ pint) beef stock (use lamb stock if using mutton)

15 ml (1 tablespoon) chopped fresh thyme

1 fresh rosemary sprig

4 potatoes, peeled and halved

15 ml (1 tablespoon) chopped fresh parsley

15 ml (1 tablespoon) chopped fresh thyme

salt and freshly ground black pepper

1. Cut the meat into bite-size chunks, removing as much fat as you like, but leave some on the meat as this will make it tender and add flavour.

2. Heat the oil in a heavy-based saucepan and add the onions, carrots, celery and swede, if using. Cook for 2 minutes and then add the meat. Cook and turn until the meat is brown on the outside, about 5–6 minutes.

3. Add the wine, stock, thyme and rosemary and seasoning. Put the potatoes on top and cover. Simmer gently until the meat is cooked, about 1 ¹/₂ hours. With mutton this takes longer, about 2–2 ¹/₄ hours.

4. While the meat is simmering, stir occasionally and remove any grease that has come to the top.

5. When the meat has cooked, add the chopped parsley and thyme and stir in. Serve with some lovely crusty bread. This is also absolutely fabulous with parsley dumplings.

Mixed Meats in Balsamic Dressing
Bollito Misto all'Aceto Balsamico

I love this dish because, firstly, it is a very healthy way of eating meat and, secondly if you are entertaining, there is hardly any work.

Serves 6   Preparation time: 30 minutes   Cooking time: 2 ½ hours

1 small cotechino (boiled pork sausage)

2 onions

2 carrots

2 celery stalks

800 g (1¾ lb) beef, preferably back, shoulder, loin or topside

400 g (14 oz) brisket

300 g (10 oz) calf's head

200 g (7 oz) calf's tongue

1 calf's foot

½ chicken

1 marrow bone

salt

balsamic vinegar, green pickle sauce or Mostarda di Cremona
(dried fruit in a mustard sauce, available from delicatessens), to serve

1. Pierce the cotechino with a fork and roll it up in wet muslin, tie both ends to make a parcel, place in cold water and simmer for about 2 hours. When it is cooked, remove from water, unwrap and keep warm.

2. Meanwhile, to a large pan containing lightly salted water, add the vegetables and bring to the boil; add the beef, brisket and calf's head and tongue and cook for 1 hour.

3. Add the remaining cuts of meat and the marrow bone and carry on cooking for another hour, at the end of which the heat should be lowered and the sausage added.

4. Carve the boiled meats and serve hot, dressed with several tablespoons of balsamic vinegar or green pickle sauce or mustard fruits.

Ossobuco My Way
Ossobuco Casa Nostra

Ossobuco is knuckle of veal. This wonderful recipe just lends itself to a great family Sunday lunch: especially served with this rice – you don't need a starter. Also you can do like my mom used to do and leave it on while you take your kids to school.

Serves 4   Preparation time: 15 minutes   Cooking time: 1 ½ hours

90 ml (3½ fl oz) olive oil

6 shallots or one large onion, chopped finely

1 fresh chilli, de-seeded and diced

4 garlic cloves, chopped finely

4 celery sticks, chopped

4 large carrots, chopped

100 g (3½ oz) plain flour, seasoned

4 ossobuco (veal knuckles)

200 ml (7 fl oz) dry white wine

2 cans of peeled, chopped tomatoes

600 ml (1 pint) meat stock

1 fresh rosemary sprig

4 bay leaves

salt and freshly ground black pepper

For the risotto:

15 ml (1 tablespoon) olive oil

200 g (7 oz) risotto rice

a glass of white wine

1.5 litres (2¾ pints) vegetable stock

200 g (7 oz) peas

a knob of butter

2 pinches of saffron strands

100 g (3 ½ oz) parmesan cheese, grated

1. You need a wide, deep pan that fits in the oven. Heat the olive oil, add half the shallots, chilli and garlic, stir with a wooden spoon and then add the celery and carrots and sauté until soft. Place the flour on a plate and roll the ossobuco in it. Place in the pan and cook for 5 minutes on each side. Add the wine and simmer for 3 minutes.

2. Add the tomatoes, meat stock, rosemary, bay leaves and seasoning and cook for 5 minutes. Place in the oven and cook for 40 minutes.

3. Meanwhile make the risotto. Start by pan-frying the remaining shallots in the olive oil, then add the rice, stirring with a wooden spoon. Add the white wine and simmer until it is all absorbed. Start adding the vegetable stock a bit at a time, making sure the rice has absorbed the liquid before adding the next lot.

4. After 5 minutes, add the peas and carry on adding the stock until it's all used; this should take about 25 minutes.

5. To finish, add the butter, saffron and parmesan and stir well. Divide between four plates and then place your ossobuco on top, with all the vegetables.

Herbs in Italian Cooking

There are certain herbs that we Italians use more than others, with the result that they have now become part of the character of our cooking.

I am sure I don't need to go into any detail on **garlic**! It is mainly used in soups, marinades and stews, with red meats and fish, and is used more in the south of Italy than the north. For all of you worried about smelling of garlic after eating, a useful tip is to eat some fresh parsley which counteracts the garlic, so no more garlic breath!

Bay leaves are used for their balsamic and penetrating smell, more to enhance other flavours than for their own flavour.

Both the flowers and sweet-smelling seeds of wild **fennel** are used in Italian cooking. The seeds are used for their aniseed-like flavour, particularly for cooking grilled fish and pork dishes.

Mint is used to heighten the flavour of salads, soups, sauces and fruit salads as well as being great for teas.

Oregano is mainly used with tomatoes, mozzarella and pizza. It has a fragrant smell and taste and is always used in pizza sauce.

Rosemary is my favourite herb; it grows practically everywhere in the Mediterranean and along the Adriatic coast. I use rosemary in just about everything, but traditionally it is used for roast lamb and pork, stews, roast potatoes and desserts. Not only does it add a great flavour to your food but it is also good for your digestion. A good idea is to use the stalks for skewers, especially with fish, to flavour the food with rosemary.

Another typical Mediterranean shrub, **sage** has a hot, spicy and slightly bitter taste which is indispensable for veal saltimbocca or calf's liver; it also goes well with grilled meats and fish, stuffings and beans.

Truffles grow deep underneath the soil. They are basically a fungus on the roots of various trees, those that develop on oak tree roots are considered to be the best. The **white truffle** has an average weight of 50–100 g (1¾-3½ oz). Its skin is pale yellow with the pulp ranging in colour from brown to pale hazelnut. It has a strong, appetising perfume and a characteristic taste which changes with cooking. Its commercial value is higher than the black and it is only gathered between 1 October and 31 December. The price ranges from £1000 to £1500 per kg.

The **black truffle** takes its name from a town situated in the mountains of Umbria (Norcia). It ranges in size from that of a walnut to a small orange, and has black skin and tiny warts. The pulp is an opaque purplish black with white veins which redden on contact with air and become black when cooked. It has a delicate aroma and a characteristic taste which does not change with cooking. These are collected from 15 November to 15 March.

Italian Hams & Salamis

The art of preserving pork meats has, over the centuries, produced hundreds of specialities which have become established in the various regions of the country.

Without a doubt, hams have become synonymous with Italian cured pork meats. They are considered to be very prestigious, with the most famous being **prosciutto di parma**. Located at the foot of the Apennine mountains, is an area constantly exposed to a dry, pure air which creates unique and ideal conditions for the natural drying of hams. By law, parma ham must be produced within a particular strip of land at the foot of the mountains in the province of Parma. Parma ham is derived from fresh thighs: once they have been refrigerated (not frozen) they are trimmed in a special way to obtain the characteristic shape of a chicken leg. The hams are rubbed with wet salt on the rind and with dry salt on the muscular parts, covered in a thin layer of sea salt and placed in refrigerated cells, where the temperature and humidity are carefully controlled. After about 7 days the hams are removed and cleaned, then lightly salted. They are refrigerated again for about 15–18 days depending on the weight; this gives the meat time to absorb the salt and release some of the moisture. When the residual salt has been washed off, the hams are 'rested' for 60–70 days, during which time the absorbed salt penetrates deeply into the joint and distributes itself evenly within the muscular mass.

After this period they are washed with tepid water and then dried in special rooms for months. The muscular part is then covered in lard, which softens the superficial layers to stop them from drying too quickly. The whole process takes 10 months and is very labour-intensive, which is why the ham is very expensive.

San Daniele proscuitto is another well known uncooked ham and the process of making it is very similar to parma ham; the main difference is that San Daniele ham is put into soft presses to obtain the guitar shape, rather than being beaten with wooden mallets like parma ham. The makers check that San Daniele ham is curing properly by inserting a sharpened horse bone into the ham and smelling it.

Bresaola is obtained from the top-quality meat of an ox or heifer. The meat is treated with salt, pepper, cinnamon, cloves and crushed garlic. The dissolved salt and the natural juices of the meat form a brine, in which the bresaola is left for a 10–15 days. It is then dried and rubbed to help the salt penetrate further, after which it is hung in a very dry place for 10 days and then in a curing shed for from one month to three.

Sausage & Borlotti Casserole with Polenta
Salsiccie Piccanti con Polenta

This is a lovely winter warmer, especially for large families. I remember that my mother had to feed the nine of us, so she came up with this dish and we used to eat it all the time because it was so inexpensive to make. She always served it with polenta, a combination that is absolutely delicious.

Serves 4   Preparation time: 15 minutes   Cooking time: 1 hour

45 ml (3 tablespoons) olive oil

8 Italian sausages

1 onion, chopped

2 garlic cloves, chopped

450 g (1 lb) carrots, diced finely

1 celery heart, diced

2 leeks, washed, chopped finely

200 ml (7 fl oz) white wine such as Sauvignon Blanc

150 ml (¼ pint) vegetable stock

1 cooking apple, cored, peeled and chopped finely

1 bay leaf

400 g can borlotti beans, drained and rinsed

5 ml (1 teaspoon) plain flour, mixed to a paste with 5 ml (1 teaspoon) soft butter

salt and freshly ground black pepper

For the polenta:

10 ml (2 teaspoons) salt

175 g (6 oz) polenta

50 g (1¾ oz) butter

100 g (3½ oz) freshly grated parmesan cheese

45 ml (3 tablespoons) chopped fresh flat-leaf parsley

1. Heat the oil in a large, deep pan. Add the sausages, onion, garlic, carrots, celery, and leeks to the pan. Stir well and cook for 10 minutes, until just turning golden brown.

2. Add the wine, stock, apple and bay leaf and season with salt and freshly ground black pepper. Bring to the boil, reduce the heat and simmer for 40 minutes, until the sausages are cooked through and the vegetables are very soft.

3. Add the beans during the final 10 minutes of cooking. If the juices need to be thickened slightly, stir in the flour paste, stirring constantly; cook for a further 1 minute.

4. Meanwhile, make the polenta. Put 1 litre (1¾ pints) of water in a large, deep pan, add the salt and bring to the boil. Reduce the heat and gradually add the polenta, stirring constantly with a whisk.

5. Simmer for 20 minutes, until the polenta is very dense and thick and separating from the side of the pan; it may seem the polenta has thickened faster than stated, but it really must cook on to allow the grains to become tender.

6. Beat the butter and parmesan into the polenta and season to taste, adding plenty of freshly ground black pepper. Stir in the parsley.

7. To serve, divide the polenta between four large, shallow bowls and spoon over the sausage and vegetable mixture. Spoon over the juices and serve.

Thinly Sliced Beef Fillet
Tagliata di Manzo

This beef dish is a winner every time; not too much cooking, simple ingredients, less is more in the recipe. Basically, you can't possibly go wrong!

Serves 4   Preparation time: 10 minutes   Cooking time: 10 minutes

350 g (12 oz) whole beef fillet

45 ml (3 tablespoons) olive oil

1 fresh rosemary sprig, tough stalks removed, leaves chopped finely

1 shallot, chopped finely

juice of 1 lime

**30 ml (2 tablespoons) Mostarda di Cremona
(dried fruit in a mustard sauce, available from delicatessens)**

salt and freshly ground black pepper

1. Preheat the oven to 220°C/fan oven 200°C/Gas Mark 7. Heat an ovenproof frying pan and then brush the meat all over with a little of the olive oil and roast for 8–10 minutes. Leave to rest for 3 minutes.

2. Put the remaining olive oil in a small bowl, stir in the rosemary, shallot and lime juice and season with salt and pepper.

3. Thinly slice the fillet steak and divide amongst the plates; spoon over the mustard fruits. Add the hot dressing and serve immediately.

Lamb Cutlets in Herbed Breadcrumbs
Cotolette d'Agnello Panate

Serves 4   Preparation time: 15 minutes   Cooking time: 15 minutes

Normally you would make this dish with veal or chicken but I tried it with lamb and it is very tasty. Make sure you flavour the breadcrumbs well. You can also serve the lamb with spaghetti and tomato sauce to make a great lunch dish.

1 garlic clove, chopped finely

1 teaspoon dried oregano

10 fresh basil leaves, chopped finely

6 fresh rosemary sprigs, tough stalks discarded and leaves chopped finely

25 g (1 oz) fresh mint, chopped finely

100 g (3½ oz) dried breadcrumbs

50 g (1¾ oz) plain flour

4 eggs

12 lamb cutlets or chops

vegetable oil, for shallow-frying

salt and freshly ground black pepper

2 lemons, sliced, to serve

1. Mix the garlic and herbs in a large dish with the breadcrumbs. Place the flour in another dish and season with salt and freshly ground black pepper. Lightly beat the eggs in another dish.

2. First coat the lamb cutlets with the flour, then the egg and finally the breadcrumbs, pressing the breadcrumbs well on to the meat.

3. Heat the oil in a large frying pan and add the lamb cutlets. Cook for 5–8 minutes on each side. Allow to stand for 2 minutes (the meat should still be rare on the inside).

4. Serve the cutlets with lemon slices.

Calves' Liver with Proscuitto, Butter & Sage
Fegato di Vitello Burro e Salvia

Serves 4   Preparation time: 10 minutes   Cooking time: 8 minutes

Liver when overcooked is quite tough, like rubber, but if it's too rare it puts people off. Make sure you cook it just enough, even if you have to cut it with a sharp knife when cooking to check how well done it is. The parma ham is optional but it does add more flavour – and why not throw in a couple of onions?

4 x 175 g (6 oz) pieces of calves' liver

30 ml (2 tablespoons) flour

4 slices of parma ham

4 fresh sage leaves

15 ml (1 tablespoon) extra-virgin olive oil

25 g (1 oz) butter

100 ml (3½ fl oz) dry white wine

juice of ½ lemon

15 ml (1 tablespoon) finely chopped fresh parsley

salt and freshly ground black pepper

1. Pat the calves' liver with a kitchen towel to remove as much liquid as you can.
2. Put the flour in a shallow dish, season with salt and pepper and then coat each piece of liver in the seasoned flour.
3. Take slices of parma ham and wrap around each piece of liver, then place a sage leaf on top of the ham and secure with a cocktail stick.
4. Heat the oil in a frying pan, add the calves' liver, cook for 2 minutes on each side and then remove.
5. Clean out the pan and add the butter to it. When the butter starts frothing, add the wine and lemon juice, bring to the boil and allow to bubble for a minute, then return the liver to the pan, spooning over the juices.
6. Cook for 1 minute and then add the parsley and cook for another minute. Serve immediately, with the juices spooned over the liver.

Vegetables

This is a great chapter with lots of my favourites – especially the **Stuffed Courgettes**. So many people tend to overcook vegetables in water, which means you lose all the goodness and vitamins they contain. Steaming vegetables is a good alternative to boiling or you can roast them with a drizzle of olive oil. Think about cutting up some **courgettes**, **aubergines**, **peppers** and so on, and placing them in a large roasting tin with sea salt, garlic cloves and olive oil. Roast them for 15 minutes and then add a little goat's cheese – what a treat!

Onion Cannelloni
Cannelloni di Cipolla

Onions have to be the most underrated vegetable on the market. They come in all sort of shapes and sizes. My other favourite way of doing this recipe is actually to use the onion layers as cannelloni, stuff them with goat's cheese and tomato and roast them for 30 minutes; but don't divert just yet, try this great recipe first.

Serves 4   Preparation time: 15 minutes
Cooking time: 1 hour, including making pancakes

For the pancakes:
225 g (8 oz) plain white flour
5 ml (1 teaspoon) salt
2 large eggs, beaten with a fork but not whisked
1 large egg yolk, beaten
350 ml (12 fl oz) milk
25 g (1 oz) unsalted butter, melted
oil, for frying

For the filling:
200 g (7 oz) unsalted butter
1 garlic clove, crushed
10 large onions, sliced thinly
90 ml (3½ fl oz) good balsamic vinegar
25 g (1 oz) fresh basil leaves, chopped finely
100 g (3½ oz) parmesan cheese, grated
salt and freshly ground black pepper
60 ml (4 tablespoons) grated parmesan cheese, for topping

1. Make the pancake batter first. Sift together the flour and salt and then add the eggs, egg yolk, milk and butter. Whisk together until smooth; pass through a sieve if lumpy. Set to one side.
2. Make the filling. Melt the butter in a pan and then add the garlic, onions and vinegar, cooking very slowly until caramelised and golden brown. This should take about 20 minutes on a low heat. Once cooked, add the basil and the parmesan. Season to taste.
3. Using a pancake pan or non-stick pan, cook the pancakes in a little oil until they are slightly golden and cooked through.
4. Take the pancakes and place a generous amount of filling inside, roll into a cylinder shape and place on a greased baking tray. Continue until you have used all the pancakes and filling. Sprinkle parmesan over the pancake rolls and place under a hot grill until the parmesan is bubbling.

Potato Gratin with Fontina Cheese
Patate Gratinate alla Fontina

Fontina is a great cheese for cooking with. I love it with veal or pork as it is just perfect for grilling. You will fall in love with the recipe for potatoes as it is just amazing. If you are like me, you will end up just eating the potatoes and forgetting about the rest of the meal.

Serves 4   Preparation time: 10 minutes   Cooking time: 1 hour

350 ml (12 fl oz) double cream

150 ml (¼ pint) whole milk

4 garlic cloves, crushed

2 fresh thyme sprigs

1 kg (2¼ lb) desiree potatoes, peeled and sliced finely

40 g (1½ oz) butter

100 g (3½ oz) fontina cheese, grated

salt and freshly ground black pepper

1. Preheat the oven to 200°C/fan oven 180°C/Gas Mark 6.
2. Slowly bring the cream, milk, garlic and thyme to the boil. Then remove the thyme.
3. Butter a non-stick dish on all sides and layer the potatoes, seasoning each layer and adding butter knobs.
4. Pour over the hot cream and sprinkle with fontina cheese. Place in the oven and bake for 1 hour. To finish off, place under a hot grill until golden and crisp.

Tempura-style Deep-fried Vegetables
Fritto di Verdura Orientale

You can deep-fry more or less any vegetable, but most of the time the secret of success is in the batter. This is one of my favourites at the moment because I try to copy lots of dishes from Japanese restaurants, as Japanese food is my second favourite.

Serves 4   Preparation time: 25 minutes   Cooking time: 25 minutes

For the tempura batter:
1 egg yolk
200 ml (7 fl oz) iced fizzy water
100 g (3½ oz) plain white flour

For the spicy tomato sauce:
25 ml (1 fl oz) olive oil
2 garlic cloves, crushed
4 shallots, diced
6 plum tomatoes, chopped
1 fresh thyme sprig
1 fresh rosemary sprig
4 long red chillies, de-seeded and chopped
30 ml (2 tablespoons) tomato purée
600 ml (1 pint) vegetable stock
salt and freshly ground black pepper

For the vegetables for tempura:
vegetable oil, for deep-frying
1 large carrot, cut in batons
2 celery sticks, cut in batons
½ cauliflower, broken into florets
1 red pepper, de-seeded and cut in batons
1 onion, cut in rings
50 g (1¾ oz) plain flour

1. First make the tempura batter. Add the egg yolk to the iced water and then stir in the flour until completely combined.
2. Make the spicy tomato sauce. Heat the oil in a medium-size pan, add the garlic, shallots and tomatoes and cook for 2 minutes; then add the thyme, rosemary, chillies and tomato purée. Stir gently and season. Add the stock and simmer for 20 minutes. Blitz in a food processor and pass through a sieve.
3. Heat a heavy-based saucepan half full of vegetable oil to 170°C. Gently coat the vegetables in the flour and tip into the tempura batter. Fry in the hot oil until golden brown. Remove and season with salt and pepper and serve immediately, with the spicy tomato sauce.

Aubergine Lasagne
Melanzane Parmiggiana

This is a great starter or main course with salad. This recipe is like making a lasagne but without the pasta: I actually prefer it this way. If you wish, you could add mince and turn it into a moussaka, Greek style; if you are a reggie then add more vegetables (courgettes or swedes) – just cut them into cubes before adding.

Serves 4   Preparation time: 25 minutes + overnight standing
Cooking time: 25 minutes

2 large, firm aubergines, cut lengthways in 4 mm (^{1}/4 inch)
    thick slices
plain flour, for coating
60 ml (4 tablespoons) olive oil, plus extra for frying aubergines
1 large garlic clove, crushed
1 carrot, sliced
1 celery stick, sliced
1 large white onion, chopped
400 g (14 oz) can chopped Italian tomatoes
1 bay leaf
450 g (1 lb) mozzarella cheese, grated (not buffalo mozzarella)
20 g (scant 1 oz) fresh basil leaves, torn
100 g (3^1/2 oz) parmesan cheese, grated
salt & freshly ground black pepper

1. Put the layers of aubergine in a colander and sprinkle with salt. Leave for 10–15 minutes to draw off excess moisture (if you can, leave the aubergine overnight). Pat dry on a kitchen towel.
2. Preheat the oven to 200°C/fan oven 180°C/Gas Mark 6.
3. Gently flour and then fry the aubergine in a little olive oil until golden brown on both sides. Place on kitchen paper to dry off the oil.
4. Place a tablespoon of the olive oil in a large saucepan and cook the garlic, carrot, celery and onion for 2–3 minutes until soft but not coloured. Add the tomatoes and bay leaf and season to taste. Gently simmer for 20 minutes.
5. To assemble, put one-third of the tomato sauce on to the bottom of a lasagne dish, add half the aubergines and half the mozzarella. Sprinkle with fresh basil and continue to assemble in this order until all ingredients are used up. Finish with a layer of parmesan and mozzarella. Bake in the oven for 20–25 minutes.

Stuffed Courgettes
Zucchine Ripiene

A great vegetarian dish, this is also a great starter. If you are not vegetarian you can add some mince or sausagemeat or even crab; in any case this vegetable contains lots of water so make sure you sprinkle with salt before cooking and leave it for a while, then wash and drain.

Serves 4   Preparation time: 10 minutes   Cooking time: 15 minutes

45 ml (3 tablespoons) olive oil

1 garlic clove, crushed

1 large spanish onion, chopped finely

4 green or yellow courgettes

1 red pepper, de-seeded and chopped finely

1 small aubergine, chopped finely

2 plum tomatoes, de-seeded and chopped

5 ml (1 teaspoon) chopped fresh oregano

100 g (3½ oz) ricotta cheese

100 g (3½ oz) parmesan cheese, grated

salt and freshly ground black pepper

1. Preheat the oven to 180°C/fan oven 160°C/Gas Mark 4.
2. In a heavy-based pan, heat the olive oil, add the garlic and onion and cook for 3–4 minutes, until soft but not coloured.
3. Take the courgettes, cut them in half and hollow out the middle, leaving the sides strong enough to hold the filling once cooked.
4. Take the insides of the courgettes, chop finely and add to the garlic and onions. Then add the pepper, aubergine, tomatoes and oregano and season to taste. Cook for about 5 minutes. Remove from the heat and mix in the ricotta cheese and half the parmesan.
5. Place the mix in the courgette shells, sprinkle with the remaining parmesan and bake for 5–6 minutes.

Mash with Spring Greens, Olive Oil, Garlic & Chilli
Purè di Verza e Patate

If you make too much of this, a great idea is to place a little olive oil in a frying pan and fry the mash and greens to make an Italian version of bubble and squeak. I didn't even know what bubble and squeak was when I created this recipe; my PA, Luisa, told me when she was typing it that this recipe reminded her of bubble and squeak!

Serves 4   Preparation time: 10 minutes   Cooking time: 25 minutes

900 g (2 lb) red desiree potatoes
200 g (7 oz) spring greens, chopped roughly
2 garlic cloves, chopped finely
1 large long red chilli, de-seeded and chopped finely
90 ml (3½ fl oz) extra-virgin olive oil
5 ml (1 teaspoon) grated nutmeg
salt and freshly ground black pepper

1. Peel and quarter the potatoes and cook in a large pan of boiling, salted water for 20 minutes or until just tender.

2. In another saucepan, blanch the roughly chopped greens – this will take 3–4 minutes – then drain.

3. While the cabbage and potatoes are cooking, mix together the garlic and chilli.

4. When the potatoes are cooked, drain well and mash them. Mix in the cooked greens, chilli, garlic and olive oil and nutmeg. Season to taste. Serve immediately.

Peas & Smoked Bacon
Piselli e Pancetta Affumicata

This recipe is the equivalent of petits pois French style. Peas are a vegetable that we don't use much any more so this is my attempt to get them back in style. Make sure you get fresh or frozen peas but not canned ones, as they will just not taste the same.

Serves 6   Preparation time: 10 minutes   Cooking time: 10 minutes

75 g (2¾ oz) **unsalted butter**

300 g (10½ oz) **baby shallots, peeled but left whole**

2 **garlic cloves, crushed**

275 g (10 oz) **smoked bacon or pancetta cubes**
   (available in supermarkets)

750 g (1 lb 10 oz) **peas in the pod, shelled, or 400 g (14 oz)**
   frozen peas (just as good)

30 ml (2 tablespoons) **olive oil**

leaves of 1 fresh mint sprig, chopped finely

salt and freshly ground black pepper

1. Melt 50 g (2 oz) of the butter in a pan, add the shallots and garlic, cook for 2 minutes, add the bacon and cook until crisp.

2. In a separate pan, bring some salted water to the boil and then cook the peas until they are just tender, about 5 minutes.

3. Add the peas to the onion and bacon mixture and stir, then add the mint. Season to taste and add the remaining butter and the olive oil. Serve immediately. If you want to, you can add some vegetable stock, just to moisten the dish.

Baked Artichoke Hearts with Smoked Mozzarella
Cuore di Carciofo con Scamorza

You find quite a lot of recipes with artichokes in this book, but I think you can never have enough of them, as this vegetable is so good for you and so versatile to cook with. The funny thing with this recipe is that I created it as a result of a mistake one day, when I had too many artichokes.

Serves 4   Preparation time: 25 minutes   Cooking time: 40 minutes

4 large artichoke hearts (see page 134 for how to prepare)
30 ml (2 tablespoons) wine vinegar
1 spanish onion, chopped finely
2 garlic cloves, crushed
45 ml (3 tablespoons) olive oil
leaves of 2 fresh basil sprigs, chopped
leaves of 1 small fresh rosemary sprig, chopped
100 g (3½ oz) breadcrumbs
200 g (7 oz) smoked mozzarella, chopped very finely
grated parmesan cheese (optional), for topping
salt and freshly ground black pepper

1. Boil the artichoke hearts in salted water with the vinegar until tender, approximately 30 minutes. Meanwhile, preheat the oven to 200°C/fan oven 180°C/Gas Mark 6.
2. Gently cook the onion and the garlic in a frying pan with half the olive oil until soft; add the chopped basil, rosemary, breadcrumbs, salt and pepper and the remaining oil.
3. Remove the artichokes from the pan and place them on a baking tray.
4. Stuff the artichokes with the onion mix and crumble the smoked mozzarella on top (you can also sprinkle some parmesan on top). Bake until melted and piping hot. (You could also cook this under a preheated grill.) Serve with a rocket salad.

Red Peppers Filled with Spaghetti
Peperoni Ripieni con Spaghetti

Serves 4   Preparation time: 30 minutes   Cooking time: 10 minutes

You normally stuff peppers with mince or other vegetables but this recipe makes a great starter and the presentation is second to none. Make sure the spaghetti is not overcooked and the sauce is not too dry, otherwise the whole thing could end up that way.

275 g (10 oz) spaghetti

60 ml (4 tablespoons) olive oil, plus extra for spaghetti

4 large red peppers

salt and ground black pepper

For the spaghetti filling:

90 ml (3½ fl oz) olive oil

1 garlic clove

1 long red chilli, de-seeded and chopped

20 g (scant 1 oz) fresh flat-leaf parsley, chopped finely

50 g (1¾ oz) parmesan cheese, grated

1. Cook the spaghetti in salted, boiling water according to pack instructions and drain well. You must drizzle the pasta with some olive oil so that it doesn't stick together and this also stops the cooking process. Preheat the oven to 200°C/fan oven 180°C/Gas Mark 6.

2. Place the whole peppers on a baking tray and drizzle with olive oil and salt and pepper. Cook until slightly soft, about 10–15 minutes.

3. Remove and place in a bowl, cover with cling film and leave to sweat for 15 minutes; this will enable you to remove the skin easily.

4. Peel and cut off the top of the pepper, leaving the rest whole, and remove the seeds. Set aside.

5. Make the filling. Heat half the oil in a heavy-based pan, add the garlic and chilli and fry gently until slightly coloured. Add the drained spaghetti, parsley and the remaining olive oil and then season. Stuff the pasta into the peppers and sprinkle with parmesan; grill until bubbling and serve immediately.

Shopping in Italian Food Markets

Just recently I had the chance to return to my home town of Pescara, where the markets are the best thing to visit. I went to the fish auction, where you bargain for your fish straight off the boats, probably the sexiest way of buying fresh fish and getting ideas for the recipes you will create. I then went to the fruit and vegetable market, where I felt like buying everything. I was actually staying at the nearby hotel but still ended up buying lots of fruit and my favourite broad beans and fresh peas. Sadly, people in this country don't go to markets enough. The supermarkets have lots to do with it by stocking everything you can possibly want. But for me the experience of exploring markets has to be much more pleasing and the fact that you will only get local regional and seasonally fresh produce at a much cheaper price just adds value to the whole experience.

One of my favourite things about living in London has to be the Portobello Road market on Saturdays, which almost seems like it has stopped time as it has been the same for over 30 years. The people there seem to be much more relaxed, wandering around with their families, tasting the foods on offer, just like it would be in Milan or any big city in Italy.

The thing about going to a market is that it is an experience; you get to meet lots of different characters and everybody looks healthy. What is amazing is that it doesn't matter how early you go to the market, the atmosphere is always electric – even when I go to Billingsgate fish market at 5.30 in the morning. The people shout and scream, the porters will run you over if you are not careful and the fish is still moving in boxes full of ice. Many times they manage to sell me fish that I never intended to buy, like shark or eels! This means I have to go back to the restaurant and create some new recipe, so the experience becomes fun and enjoyable. Now I have explained why, off you go to the market and get shopping!

Christmas

The Italian Christmas, as I remember it, is very different from the English. On Christmas Eve we always played cards and drank **lots of red wine** with roasted chestnuts. Then the brave ones would go to **Midnight mass**. On Christmas morning it was compulsory to go to church, or you wouldn't be allowed any lunch. My dad was very strict because one of my brothers was a priest. After mass we would go home for lunch. Presents were never a big thing but we would write a little letter and place it under Mom or Dad's plate and hope they would give us some money. The most important thing in those days was to be happy and to spend lots of **time together as a family**.

Roast Suckling Pig
Porchetta

Serves 6–8   Preparation time: 20 minutes   Cooking time: 40 minutes

You might have trouble finding the right size pig for this recipe, in which case try Pugh's Piglets (tel 01995 602571). Alternatively, you could substitute a whole loin of pork. Now in my village in Italy, people roast the whole pig and then sell it on the side of the street out of their vans ... like a hog roast – and that is where the name porchetta comes from. Serve with roast potatoes and green beans.

1 small suckling pig
300 ml (½ pint) olive oil
1 onion, halved
3 carrots, halved
3 garlic cloves
2 bunches of fresh rosemary
3 cooking apples, peeled
30 ml (2 tablespoons) brown sugar
300 ml (½ pint) pork stock
½ bottle of good white wine
25 g (1 oz) butter
salt

1. Once you have got the pig, to make sure it cooks properly and more quickly, split it in half, leaving the head on if possible, or get your butcher to do this for you.

2. Preheat the oven to 180°C/fan oven 160°C/Gas Mark 4.

3. Place some olive oil in a large roasting tin and heat. When hot, place the pig in it with the halved onion and carrots, whole garlic cloves, rosemary and one of the apples, quartered. Place in the hot oven and roast for 40 minutes, depending on the size of the pig (approximately 15 minutes per 450 g/1 lb) and 20 minutes extra. Leave to rest for at least 15 minutes before carving.

4. Wash and slice the remaining apples thinly, sprinkle with brown sugar and place under the grill until golden brown.

5. Take the suckling pig and cut it into pieces – to make them crisp, place each portion under a hot grill for 3 minutes.

6. Using the pan you cooked the suckling pig in, add the stock with the wine and the butter and simmer for 5–8 minutes. To make a good gravy, strain everything into a small pan and bring to the boil.

7. When serving, place the pig in the middle of the plate, add slices of glazed apple on top, and put some roast potatoes on one side and green beans on the other – serve the gravy separately.

Rosemary Roast Potatoes
Patate al Rosmarino

Rosemary grows everywhere but it is not used in English cooking very much. It is a great herb for vegetables, fish and lamb. My favourite way is to use the rosemary sticks as skewers for fish or chicken (page 128), as this infuses the food with rosemary flavour and looks great on the plate.

Serves 4   Preparation time: 10 minutes   Cooking time: 1 hour

4 large king edward potatoes, peeled and cut in quarters
4 tablespoons semolina
200 ml (7 fl oz) olive oil
2 garlic cloves, unpeeled
2 fresh rosemary sprigs
salt and freshly ground black pepper

1. Preheat the oven to 200°C/fan oven 180°C/Gas Mark 6. Bring a large pan of water to the boil and add the potatoes; par-boil for 5 minutes and then drain.

2. Put the semolina, salt and pepper into a dish, mix well and toss the potatoes in this until fully coated.

3. Place the oil in a large, deep roasting pan and place in the oven to get hot. Then add potatoes, garlic cloves and rosemary sprigs and roast the potatoes for an hour or until golden brown. Remove the garlic and rosemary before serving.

Spinach with Garlic & Chilli
Spinaci Aglio e Olio

Spinach is a very versatile vegetable, great in salads and equally good with roast meat or fish. This recipe works really well as it gives a little kick: spinach on its own can be a little bland.

Serves 4   Preparation time: 5 minutes   Cooking time: 10 minutes

1.25 kg (2³/₄ lb) spinach, washed and tough stalks removed
45 ml (3 tablespoons) olive oil
2 garlic cloves, crushed
1 fresh red chilli, de-seeded and chopped finely
salt and freshly ground black pepper

1. Place the spinach leaves in a large, heavy-based saucepan (do not add any water). Cover the pan and cook gently for 6–7 minutes until the spinach wilts, stirring occasionally to keep it from sticking. Drain well and allow to cool slightly, and then squeeze out excess water. Chop roughly.

2. Heat the oil in the same pan. Stir in the garlic and chilli and fry for 2 minutes. Replace the spinach, season to taste and cook until the spinach is heated through. Serve immediately.

Artichoke Lasagne
Lasagna ai Carciofi

Serves 4   Preparation time: 30 minutes   Cooking time: 25–30 minutes

During my last visit to my family, my sister-in-law made this fantastic dish for me and my friends and not only did I ask for the recipe, so did everyone else. When artichoke is in season it has to be the best vegetable to cook and eat; sadly, very few people know how to prepare and cook it. Marinating artichokes in some olive oil, garlic and herbs is simple and delicious as a starter or antipasto.

60ml (4 tablespoons) olive oil

1 large garlic clove, crushed

1 large white onion, chopped

2 x 400 g cans of chopped Italian tomatoes

100 ml (3½ fl oz) good Italian red wine

6 globe artichokes, prepared and cooked (page 134)

175 g (6 oz) no-pre-cook lasagne sheets

450 g (1 lb) mozzarella cheese, grated

a large handful of fresh basil leaves, torn

salt and freshly ground black pepper

1. Preheat the oven to 200°C/fan oven 180°C/Gas Mark 6.

2. Place a tablespoon of the olive oil in a large saucepan and cook the garlic and onions for 2–3 minutes, until soft but not coloured. Add the tomatoes and wine and season to taste. Gently simmer for 20 minutes.

3. Remove all the outside leaves from the artichokes to leave the hearts. Slice the artichoke hearts into three horizontally. In a pan, heat the rest of the olive oil and gently fry the cooked artichoke slices for approximately 1–2 minutes on each side.

4. To assemble the lasagne, put one-third of the tomato sauce in the bottom of the lasagne dish and add a layer of lasagne sheets, then add a little more sauce. Add half the artichokes and half the mozzarella. Sprinkle with fresh basil and continue to assemble in this order until all ingredients are used up, finishing with a layer of cheese. Bake in the oven for 20–25 minutes.

Black Pudding with Pancetta, Walnut & Lamb's Lettuce
Sanguinaccio alle Noci e Pancetta

Black pudding, when I was a kid, would only be available at Christmas, when my dad would kill a pig and everything from that animal was used to feed my large family. That included black pudding; then it was a necessity for us but nowadays it is quite a trendy dish.

Serves 4   Preparation time: 5 minutes   Cooking time: 12 minutes

400 g (14 oz) black pudding, cut into 8 slices

8 slices of pancetta

50 ml (2 fl oz) extra-virgin olive oil, plus extra for frying

100 g (3½ oz) whole peeled walnuts

juice of 1 lemon

125 g (4 ½ oz) lamb's lettuce

a small bunch of fresh chives, snipped

20 ml (4 teaspoons) white wine vinegar

salt and freshly ground black pepper

1. Place the slices of black pudding on a baking tray and then put under a hot grill for 2 minutes on each side, until cooked. Keep warm.
2. Take the sliced pancetta and cook on another baking tray under the grill until crisp. Pat both the black pudding and pancetta with kitchen paper to remove any fat. Keep warm.
3. Place a little olive oil in a frying pan and gently pan-fry the walnuts. Be careful not to burn them.
4. To make the dressing, take the lemon juice, remaining olive oil, salt and pepper and mix together. Dress the lamb's lettuce with half the dressing. Add the walnuts and chives to the remaining dressing.
5. To arrange on a plate, put the black pudding and the pancetta on first, then the salad on top and finally the walnuts; drizzle over the dressing. Serve immediately.

Cooked Cream with Fruits of the Forest
Pannacotta ai Fruitti di Bosco

The translation of pannacotta is 'cooked cream', which is exactly what it is, but what makes this recipe great is adding the marsala, which I am convinced is going to make a big comeback. If you remember, it was used only in zabaglione but it is now being used in many other dishes. A good idea is to invest in a quality marsala that would be great for cooking or as an apéritif (a bit like sherry or dessert wine). If you like, you can substitute a little melted chocolate for the berries, for those chocoholics out there.

Serves 4   Preparation time: 20 minutes
Cooking time: 10 minutes + chilling overnight

4 tablespoons caster sugar
300 ml (½ pint) double cream
300 ml (½ pint) milk
1 vanilla pod, halved lengthways
175 g (6 oz) mascarpone cheese
30 ml (2 tablespoons) marsala
2 teaspoons gelatine granules
sunflower oil, for brushing

For the berries:
100 g (3½ oz) caster sugar
finely grated zest of 1 lime
juice of ½ lime
2 fresh mint sprigs
150 g (5½ oz) winter berries, e.g. frozen forest fruits

1. Simmer the sugar, cream, milk and vanilla pod for 5–8 minutes, stirring occasionally. Remove the vanilla pod, rinse clean and store to use again.
2. Remove the pan from the heat and whisk the mascarpone into the hot cream. Put the marsala into a bowl and stir in the gelatine granules. Leave to swell. Then sit the bowl over boiling water and stir until the gelatine has dissolved. Mix into the warm cream.
3. Lightly oil four 200 ml (7 fl oz) ramekins or glass pots and pour in the cream. Chill for 3 hours or overnight until set.
4. To turn out the pannacottas, dip each ramekin in a bowl of hot water for 30 seconds and turn on to serving plates or bowls, giving them a good shake to release.
5. About 30 minutes before serving, make the fruit compote. Dissolve the sugar in 50 ml (2 fl oz) of water and then boil for 1 minute. Allow the syrup to cool for 5 minutes before adding the lime zest, juice, mint and fruit. Leave to cool. Discard the mint sprigs and then spoon the fruits and syrup around the pannacottas to serve.

Italian Feasts

When in Italy, eat like the Italians do and look healthy. You can still eat a feast in the smallest and cheapest restaurant in the middle of nowhere, starting with crostini, mixed salamis and cheeses, then pasta or gnocchi or both, moving on to meat or fish with potatoes and salads. Luckily enough we are not big on desserts! So it is seasonal fruit to finish. Italians are very aware of seasonal food – you would not catch an Italian ordering strawberries in December in a restaurant; neither would a good restaurant serve out of season food, except the ones that cater for tourists. So when you go to Rome or Milan or any big city, try to avoid the ones with an English or German translation on the menus and ask your hotel for a restaurant with local specialities; these normally have no menus but you will end up with a feast at very little expense.

My latest visit to my beautiful region of Abruzzo, where all my seven brothers and one sister still live, was amazing. One night I decided to entertain 15 of my family and so my brother took us to a restaurant 20 minutes' drive from the sea; you would need a serious local map to find it! As we arrived, the antipasti started coming and by the time the pasta appeared I was very full, but the duck sauce on the pappardelle was out of this world and then there were roast meats and limoncello (lemon liqueur) with lots of home-made wine. Everything is home-made here and at £90 for 15 people, to say I would go back at the drop of hat is an understatement.

Weddings in Italy have a reputation as occasions for stuffing yourself with food. I remember going to receptions with my parents and my mother always took a bagful of food home at the end of the lunch — a bit embarrassing, but nevertheless providing another feast for the family the following day, free of charge. As money was quite tight and she had nine children to feed, it was understandable. Even now, in my village, weddings are still feasts and I can't wait for one of my 25 nephews and nieces to get married so I can go back to Italy and stuff myself with fantastic food.

Desserts

Us Italians have never been big on desserts. In the morning we might have a **cornetto** or **bombolone** with an espresso; after lunch we always have fruit. Sometimes on special occasions my mom or my sister-in-law made a cake and we had **cantuccini** or **cioccolatini** with coffee. Things like **tiramisù** or zabaglione, which you order in Italian restaurants in England, were never very common in Italy. Even now there are very few restaurants in Italy that provide a selection of desserts.

Neapolitan Cake
Pastiera Napoletana

OK, I agree, not the simplest and quickest of recipes in this book, but the reward is fantastic if you have a go, and you can keep this cake for a few days.

Serves 12

Preparation time: 1 hour + 8 days soaking

Cooking time: 3 hours

For the pastry:
300 g (10 oz) 00-grade white flour
150 g (5 oz) fresh lard
150 g (5 oz) caster sugar
3 eggs

For the filling:
225 g (8 oz) whole wheat (available from delicatessens)
500 ml (18 fl oz) milk
½ lemon, peel only
2 pinches of ground cinnamon
200 g (7 oz) caster sugar
a pinch of salt
500 g (1 lb 2 oz) fresh ricotta cheese
40 ml (scant 3 tablespoons) orange-flower water
75 g (2¾ oz) candied orange and lemon peel, chopped finely
6 egg yolks
6 egg whites, whisked stiffly
icing sugar

1. Put the whole wheat in a bowl, cover with water and soak for 8 days, changing the water daily. At the end of this time, drain well, transfer to a saucepan, cover with water and boil for 15 minutes. Drain the wheat and return to the pan; set to one side.
2. Preheat the oven to 180°C/fan oven 160°C/Gas Mark 4. Heat the milk to boiling point. Pour the milk over the wheat and add the lemon peel, a pinch of cinnamon, a teaspoon of the sugar and a pinch of salt. Simmer for about 2 hours until the wheat has absorbed all the milk; remove the lemon peel.
3. Prepare the shortcrust pastry. Sift the flour and add all the ingredients, combining by rubbing in with your fingers in the normal way, until the mixture is soft and well bound. Shape into a ball and refrigerate.
4. Pass the ricotta through a sieve, allowing it to drop into a large bowl. Add the remaining sugar, cinnamon, the orange-flower water and the candied fruits. Mix well and add the egg yolks, one at a time, stirring carefully.

Add the grain and then fold in the stiffly whisked egg whites.

5. Grease a 32 cm (12½ inch) cake tin with lard. Divide the pastry in half and roll out half with a rolling pin to produce a disc which will cover the bottom and the sides of the cake tin.

6. Pour the prepared mixture into the tin and shake until the mixture is level.

7. Roll out the second half of shortcrust pastry, cut into strips 1 cm (½ inch) wide and lay them in a criss-cross pattern over the filling, tucking in the edges of the pastry. Bake for an hour.

8. When the pastiera is cooked, leave to cool in the tin and then sprinkle with icing sugar; serve without removing it from the tin. This cake is much better after being kept for a few days.

Confectioner's Custard
Crema Pasticcera

Serves 12 (makes 1 litre/1 ¾ pints)

1 litre (1¾ pints) milk
350 g (12 oz) caster sugar
grated zest of 1 lemon
1 vanilla pod
6 egg yolks
a pinch of salt
125 g (4½ oz) plain flour

1. Pour a small cup of milk from the litre and put the rest into a saucepan with half of the sugar, lemon zest and vanilla pod and heat slowly until boiling.

2. In the meantime, lightly whisk the egg yolks and the pinch of salt in a bowl to break them. Sift the flour into the bowl, whisking gently and making sure that no lumps form, then whisk in the remaining sugar, and finally the remaining small cup of milk. Whisk until smooth.

3. By this time the milk should be almost boiled. Remove the vanilla pod (wipe clean in order to re-use) and lemon zest, and then pour the milk on to the egg mixture, whisking briskly whilst doing so. Return the mixture to the heat and bring to the boil, stirring with a wooden spoon all the time. As the mixture boils it will begin to get thicker, and then suddenly go very thick. At this point it is ready and you need to remove the saucepan from the heat and cool the mixture as quickly as possible. A good way to do this is to place the base of the saucepan into cold or iced water and stir the mixture gently so that a skin does not form as it cools.

Nan's Cake
Torta della Nonna

My nan lived until she was 95 years old. I didn't spend a lot of time with her, but the little time I did see her, she always offered me this great crusty cake with coffee, God bless her.

Serves 12   Preparation time: 30 minutes   Cooking time: 1 hour

500 g (1 lb 2 oz) sweet shortcrust pastry

50 g (1³/₄ oz) pine nuts

50 g (1³/₄ oz) raisins, blanched

50 ml (2 fl oz) rum

500 ml (18 fl oz) crema pasticcera (see page 189)

1 egg, beaten

vanilla sugar, to serve

1. Preheat the oven to 180°C/fan oven 160°C/Gas Mark 4. Roll out half the pastry and cut out a disc with a diameter of about 25 cm (10 inches). Transfer to a baking sheet.
2. Mix the pine nuts, raisins and rum with crema pasticcera.
3. Spread the mixture over the shortcrust pastry to form a dome shape.
4. Roll out the remaining pastry large enough to cover the dome. Press the edges together and cut it neatly.
5. Brush with the egg and pierce a few times with a fork.
6. Bake in the preheated oven for about an hour or until golden. Remove and let it cool. Transfer to a plate, sprinkle with vanilla sugar and serve.

Sparkling Sorbet
Sorbetto all'Asti Spumante

*Simple and summery,
this is very impressive –
especially if you like
Asti Spumante, and
personally I love it. To
make sugared grapes,
boil some sugar in a
little water to make a
caramel. Dip the
grapes in the caramel
and leave to set.*

Serves 6   Preparation time: 30 minutes

350 g (11½ oz) caster sugar
350 ml (11 fl oz) water
½ bottle Asti Spumante
juice of ½ lemon
1 egg white, whisked

To garnish:
fresh mint leaves
sugared white grapes (see note)

1. Place the sugar and water in a heavy-based saucepan and cook over a gentle heat until reduced by half.
2. Combine the sugar syrup, Asti Spumante and lemon juice in a food processor.
3. Pour the mixture into an ice cream mould, cover and leave in the freezer for about an hour or until it is partly solid.
4. Return the mixture to the processor and blend together with the whisked egg white until it turns light and frothy.
5. Pour back into the ice cream mould, cover and freeze.
6. Serve within 2–3 hours, garnished with mint leaves and sugared white grapes.

Cannoli alla Sicilana

Sicilians are the best at
cakes and sweets and
this is a brilliant
example. Try and find
cannoli already made
so you will just need to
fill them – much easier
for you. But if you do
make them, make extra
and freeze them until
the next time. You can
buy cannoli moulds
from good cook shops.
This recipe makes four
large cannoli.

Serves 4   Preparation time: 30 minutes + overnight resting
Cooking time: 10 minutes

For the cannoli:
250 g (9 oz) plain flour
25 g (1 oz) unsalted butter
40 g (1½ oz) caster sugar
a pinch of salt
100 ml (3 ½ fl oz) white wine
**   or marsala**
2 egg yolks
5 ml (1 teaspoon) olive oil
vegetable oil, for deep-frying

For the filling:
250 g (9 oz) ricotta cheese
50 g (1¾ oz) candied fruits
leaves of 2 fresh mint sprigs,
**   chopped finely**
10 ml (2 teaspoons) sugar
35 ml (2 tablespoons + 1 teaspoon)
**   coffee liqueur**

1. Sieve the flour, sugar and salt on to a work surface. Rub the butter into the flour and sugar. Make a well in the middle.

2. Whisk the wine in a bowl with the egg yolks and pour into the well. Using your fingers, gradually bring the flour into the liquid until a smooth dough is forming. Drizzle olive oil on to the surface to help form the dough and keep it moist. Shape the dough into a ball, wrap in cling film and leave to rest in the fridge for 24 hours.

3. Next day, work the dough by kneading it and then shape into a ball and divide into four. Cover the other three balls whilst shaping the first piece so that the dough does not dry out.

4. Flatten the dough slightly with a rolling pin or by hand, until about 2 mm thick. Cut into a rectangle on a lightly floured surface, large enough to wrap around a large cannoli mould until the edges meet. Press them together to make a cylinder. Repeat until you have covered all four moulds.

5. In a deep-fryer, carefully heat vegetable oil to 180°C and deep-fry the cannoli, still on their moulds, until golden brown. Remove with a spoon to a plate lined with kitchen paper. When cooled slightly, remove from the moulds and allow to cool.

6. Mix together all the ingredients for the filling in a bowl.

7. When the cannoli are cold, add the filling and serve at once.

Italian Liqueurs

In my experience, we Italians always tend to finish a meal with 'something for the digestion'. This is usually a shot of a liqueur called **Amaro** which is bitter in taste. If you are very brave, then try **Fernet Branca**, strong in taste, but great for settling indigestion.

The most well known liqueur is probably **Sambuca**, which in Italy we drink with an espresso; here in the UK it is normally drunk topped with a coffee bean and lit, which produces an invisible flame. There is really no point in burning the sambuca, though, as all you are doing is getting rid of the alcohol which makes the whole purpose of drinking it useless, but you can flame your panettone at Christmas with it as well. Sambuca is also great on the rocks or to dress your fruit salad; it has a liquorice flavour, is full of sugar and has a high viscosity. What makes it different from normal aniseed–flavoured drinks is the addition of elderberries.

Northern Italians drink **grappa** as the English drink brandy and, like brandy, there are various grades of grappa, from basic varieties to a Rémy Martin equivalent. Grappa is made from the stems and skins of grapes that remain after the wine is made; you can get another drink called **aqua vita** ('water of the vine'), which is made from the juice of grapes, with many Italians arguing about which is the best. Like wine, grappa is one of the most characteristic and typical products of my country and, in the last few years, it has adopted a very important role in Italian culture. In the old days it was used as a remedy for illness but in modern times it is much more of a party drink, especially after dinner. I love it just cold from the fridge. I have had some great grappa and amazing aqua vita so, as far as I am concerned, it depends on you and whether you are willing to spend a bit more to get a superior product.

Amaretto is one of those drinks you either hate or love; it has a distinct flavour of almonds although it is made with apricot kernels. This liqueur hails from a town called Saronno in Italy, where there are several distilleries which produce their own amaretto. The great thing about this liqueur is the story that goes with it. The story starts in 1525, when a student of the Leonardo Da Vinci school of art was commissioned by the Santa Maria delle Grazie in Saronno to paint a fresco of the Madonna. Being talented and passionate, he searched for many weeks for the perfect model and he finally found a young, beautiful innkeeper. During the months that followed they worked in very intimate surroundings and the young woman fell deeply in love. As a token of her love she created a sweet, almond-flavoured liqueur for him; this was the first bottle of amaretto. Amaretto is best drunk on the rocks or even in coffee and topped with cream, almost like an Irish coffee.

Lemons are in season all year round in Capri, and this is the staple for the drink that is made on the island, **limoncello**. This is a strong apéritif which can burn the back of unsuspecting throats. There is now a brand that has cream in it, which is delicious, if a bit sickly in hot weather. Limoncello should be kept in the freezer and served in shot glasses, although it is to be sipped.

Italian Coffee

It is thought that 83% of Italians drink coffee and 75% drink it every day! Which is an amazing statistic. Most of the coffee sold in Italy is Arabica or Robusta coffee, the first variety being of a higher quality.

Wherever your coffee comes from, you must choose a good quality and make sure it is fresh. Coffee from Kenya, Colombia, India, Sumatra and Guatemala is always of the best quality and always fresh. As with good wine, once you have tasted the best coffees of the world, you will never forget the experience.

Coffee, as we all know, is a stimulant and it is essential to giving me a kick start to the day – one cup of **espresso** and I am raring to go! The preparation of a good espresso starts with a careful blend of the two varieties in order to retain the right flavour, and then the heat of the water and how quickly it comes out of the machine come into play.

There are two main styles of roasting, the **Continental** or **dark roast** and the **English** or **light roast**. Roasting cannot improve the quality of the beans, though it can spoil them. The Continental roast is the one used for espresso coffee and is a taste that people like because they are used to it. In the English style, the aim is to roast the beans so that the essential oils will readily transfer to the hot water when it is added – but not too much, otherwise they will lose their flavour and aroma.

The instant variety of coffee is not used much: with a café on every corner there is no need for it. Most Italians are happy with their espresso or **cappuccino**; and in the summer you can get a **granita**, which is a glass of crushed ice with coffee poured over it, some ice cream and sugar, fantastic for getting your caffeine fix in a different way.

Nectarines in Vanilla Syrup with Rosemary-scented Mascarpone
Pescanoce al Rosmarino e Mascarpone

My love for rosemary carries on even into desserts. You must have a go at this recipe, it is quite different in taste and flavour.

Serves 6   Preparation time: 10 minutes   Cooking time: 20 minutes

small fresh rosemary sprig

60 ml (4 tablespoons) single cream

250 g (9 oz) mascarpone cheese

15 ml (1 tablespoon) icing sugar

175 g (6 oz) granulated sugar

2 vanilla pods, split

12 ripe but still firm nectarines, halved and stoned

1. Strip the leaves off the rosemary twigs and finely chop. Mix together the cream, mascarpone, icing sugar and rosemary. Cover and place in the fridge until needed.

2. In a saucepan, gently heat 500 ml (18 fl oz) of water, the granulated sugar and vanilla pods until the sugar has dissolved and then bring to the boil. Add the nectarines and simmer, covered, for 15 minutes or until the nectarines are tender.

3. Using a slotted spoon, remove the nectarines and set aside. Rapidly boil the cooking liquid for about 5 minutes or until reduced to a syrup and then pour over the nectarines. Serve warm with a spoonful of mascarpone mixture in each nectarine half.

Tiramisu with Amaretto

This very famous recipe is the classic of Italian desserts. It is good to keep it for 12 hours before eating as the flavours become better, so make it for Sunday lunch on Saturday and enjoy.

Serves 6   Preparation time: 20 minutes + 2 hours chilling

90 ml (3 ½ fl oz) very hot strong Italian coffee

45 ml (3 tablespoons) amaretto liqueur

20 sponge fingers

6 eggs, separated

165 g (5 ¾ oz) caster sugar

325 ml (10 ½ fl oz) double cream

500 g (1 lb 2 oz) mascarpone cheese

30 ml (2 tablespoons) vanilla essence

45 ml (3 tablespoons) bitter chocolate cocoa powder

1. Combine the coffee and amaretto and dip half the sponge fingers quickly in the mixture; do not allow to soak. Then lay on the bottom of a square flat dish.

2. In a heatproof bowl over a pan of simmering water, whisk the egg yolks and the sugar, remove from the heat and beat until doubled in volume, creamy and pale.

3. In a separate bowl, whisk the egg whites until they form stiff peaks.

4. In another bowl, whisk the cream until thick.

5. Gradually add the mascarpone cheese to the beaten yolks, folding it in
carefully with a wooden spoon, and then add the vanilla essence. Fold in the
cream and then the egg whites, one-third at a time, carefully.

6. Pour half the mixture over the soaked sponge fingers. Add another layer of
fingers and then cover with the rest of cheese mix.

7. Cover with cling film and refrigerate for 2 hours.

8. Remove the cling film, and then completely coat the top of the tiramisù with
the bitter cocoa powder.

Baked Honey & Ricotta Cheesecake
Torta di Ricotta al Miele

Serves 4   Preparation time: 10 minutes   Cooking time: 30 minutes

Cakes and desserts are not my best thing to cook, but I reckon if you stick to simplicity it will work every time, just like it has for me.

You could substitute another cheese here for ricotta, if you wish, but make sure it is quite bland, soft and creamy.

75 g (2¾ oz) **caster sugar**

75 g (2¾ oz) **unsalted butter, softened**

2 **eggs, separated**

75 g (2¾ oz) **self-raising flour, sifted**

60 ml (4 tablespoons) **cornflour, sifted**

5 ml (1 teaspoon) **baking powder**

a pinch of salt

For the topping:

500 g (1 lb 2 oz) **ricotta cheese**

5 **eggs**

100 ml (3½ fl oz) **liquid honey**

a pinch of ground cinnamon

50 g (1¾ oz) **candied fruit, chopped**

grated zest of 2 lemons

10 ml (2 teaspoons) **marsala**

1. Preheat the oven to 180°C/fan oven 160°/Gas Mark 4. Whisk together the sugar, butter and egg yolks until light and creamy. Then add the flour, cornflour, baking powder and salt to the creamy mix, a little at a time, beating continuously.

2. Beat the egg whites until very stiff and then gently fold into the cake mixture.

3. Grease a high-sided cake tin that either has a push-up bottom or sprung sides, and then flour the tin. Shake out any excess flour. Pour in the cake mix and bake for 25 minutes.

4. Push the ricotta through a sieve into a bowl. Separate three of the egg yolks from the egg whites, retaining both the whites and the yolks. Add two whole eggs, the three egg yolks, honey, cinnamon, candied fruits and grated lemon zest to the ricotta and combine well.

5. Beat the egg whites until stiff and then fold in the marsala.

6. The sponge should be almost cooked by this time. Reduce the oven temperature to 150°C/fan oven 130°/Gas Mark 2.

7. Pour the cheesecake mix on top of the sponge and cook for another 2–5 minutes. Allow to cool a little before removing from tin.

Panettone with Cream & Fruit Sauce
Panettone alla Frutta e Crema

Panettone is usually eaten at Christmas time and, if you invest in a really good one, you will realise why we eat so much of it. There are many different flavours, such as chocolate, vanilla and so on, but my favourite is the classic pannetone eaten with a nice caffè latte for breakfast.

Serves 8   Preparation time: 5 minutes   Cooking time: 15 minutes

250 g (9 oz) frozen whole forest fruits

100 g (3½ oz) caster sugar

100 ml (3½ fl oz) vin santo

4 amaretti biscuits, crushed

50 g (1¾ oz) unsalted butter

8 small panettone, sliced

30 ml (2 tablespoons) brandy

300 ml (½ pint) double cream

25 g (1 oz) icing sugar, plus extra to dust

1. Place the fruits in a pan with the caster sugar and vin santo. Simmer for 5 minutes. Stir in the amaretti biscuits.

2. Meanwhile, melt the butter in a frying pan and add the panettone. Fry briefly on both sides. Heat the brandy in a small pan. Pour the brandy into the frying pan and set it alight to flambé the panettone.

3. Place the cream in a large bowl and whisk with the icing sugar until soft peaks form. In another bowl, put the fruit mixture. Put the panettone into a third bowl.

4. Put all the bowls on to the table so that your guests can put the dessert together themselves, by topping the panettone with cream and then with fruit sauce.

5. Sprinkle with icing sugar as the final touch.

Walnut & Coffee Mousse
Mousse al Caffe e Noci

Walnuts were always available in my younger days, purely because we had a big tree in the garden and there were only so many walnuts we could eat, so my mom and I made this mousse one day. This has to be a great way to finish a meal. For a richer, darker mousse, omit the whipped cream.

Serves 4   Preparation time: 10 minutes

Cooking time: 10 minutes + 1 hour chilling

100 ml (3½ fl oz) strong espresso coffee

225 g (8 oz) Valrohna chocolate

125 g (4½ oz) butter

2 egg yolks

3 egg whites

25 g (1 oz) caster sugar

50 ml (2 fl oz) double cream, lightly whipped to soft peaks

25 g (1 oz) walnuts, crushed

1. Boil the coffee in a saucepan to reduce it by half, and leave to cool.

2. In a heatproof bowl over a pan of simmering water, melt the chocolate and butter, stirring gently, until completely melted.

3. Take off the heat and add the coffee reduction, stirring continuously until cooled slightly. Add the egg yolks and stir until smooth.

4. In a separate bowl, whisk the egg whites until they form soft peaks, then whisk in the sugar.

5. Stir a quarter of the egg whites into the chocolate to lighten the mix, then fold this mixture into the remaining egg whites using a metal spoon, followed by the whipped cream.

6. Gently fold in the walnuts and pour into serving glasses. Refrigerate for an hour before serving, with cream if you like.

Italian Patisserie

In Italy, the dessert course is not the most popular, but in the bars you tend to get lots of different small cakes and pastries, from chocolate biscuits to **cornetti** filled with crème pâtissière (confectioner's custard) to almond biscuits such as **cantuccini** or **amaretti**.

Different regions have different traditions, especially at Christmas or Easter. I remember Christmas time was the best time of the year because there were so many of us. Mom used to make cantuccini and we would soak them in vin santo, which is a sweet dessert wine. My mother also used to make chestnut cookies, with chestnuts, almonds, chocolate and coffee all mixed together and then fried – not very healthy I know, but they tasted great. You cannot mention Christmas without mentioning **panettone**, which is as traditional to us as fruit cake is to the English. Panettone is a bulky cylindrical cake, the largest part of which is dome-shaped; the texture is soft and coarse and it is made with natural yeast and left to rise twice when being prepared. The traditional variety contains raisins and candied fruit. You can now get various special panetonne, covered in almond icing or filled either with zabaglione, hazelnut or liqueur cream.

Pandoro is another Christmas cake and it is very similar in size and shape to the panettone but is recognised by its characteristic deep vertical groove all along the sides. This cake differs from panettone in that it includes cocoa butter and does not have any fruit; it is normally served with a layer of icing sugar.

Torrone, which is also eaten at Christmas, was created in Cremona in AD 1600. It is made from a blend of honey, almonds and egg whites and is usually marketed in bars slightly longer and thicker than chocolate bars; it is very similar to nougat.

During the Easter period no Italian household is complete without a **Colomba**. This sweet is shaped like a dove and is made with flour, butter, eggs and candied orange peel. It is coated in almond icing and liberally decorated with almonds and granulated sugar. An overdose of sugar for us Italians before and after fasting.

It is worth noting that most Italians easily refuse sweets at the end of a meal as we tend to have three courses before the dessert. I will only eat desserts on family occasions or feast days.

Breakfast, as I remember, would have been a cappuccino or caffe latte with **bombolone**, which nobody has recreated in the UK yet. It looks like a doughnut but is stuffed with a kind of custard cream and deep-fried, then dusted with sugar. It is probably the thing I miss most from my childhood.